M 738

CAPTAIN COOK NAMING QUEEN CHARLOTTE'S SOUND

# The Life and Voyages
of
# Captain James Cook

### Selections
## With Introductions and Notes

**BY**

## C. G. CASH, F.R.S.G.S.

Geography Master at the Edinburgh Academy

## Illustrated by Paul Hardy

## BLACKIE AND SON LIMITED
### LONDON GLASGOW DUBLIN BOMBAY

# CONTENTS

i

# ILLUSTRATIONS

# INTRODUCTION

James Cook was born at Marton, in North York-shire, on October 27th, 1728. As a youth he was apprenticed to a shopkeeper in a sea-side village near Whitby, but ran away to sea when he was fourteen years old. For some years he served in a collier, but in 1755, when war broke out with France, he entered the Royal Navy, and remained in the service till his death in 1779.

He spent some years off the American coast, engaged in important surveying work, and during this time studied all things that might make him a better seaman and a capable officer. He had charge of the naval portion of the expedition that resulted in the capture of Quebec in 1759, and was recognized by his superiors as a man of great ability and value.

The three famous voyages of which accounts are given in this book rank very high among scientific explorations. They added greatly to our knowledge of the Southern and Pacific Oceans, settled for a time the question of the "Great Southern Continent", and made New Zealand and Australia known to us. At the time more was thought of the discovery of the Sandwich Islands, but this was probably on account of Cook's death there. We have since learned how very much greater is the value of our antipodes. But perhaps the greatest benefit Cook conferred on the world was his showing that a ship's crew could remain at sea for a long time, and yet avoid the dreaded scurvy by proper attention to food and cleanliness. Before his time no ship was at sea for many months without losing some of her crew from this disease; since his lesson has been learned, scurvy has ceased to be the seaman's scourge.

# THE LIFE AND VOYAGES OF CAPTAIN JAMES COOK

## THE FIRST VOYAGE, 1768–1771

In June, 1769, a transit of Venus was to occur; that is, the planet Venus was to pass between the Earth and the Sun, and would be seen as a dark spot moving across the face of the Sun. By careful observations of this phenomenon astronomers are able to measure the size and distance of the Sun. It was therefore decided by the government and the Royal Society to send out an expedition to the South Pacific to make such observations, and of this expedition Cook was placed in command.

He was instructed to remain at Tahiti, one of the recently-discovered Society Islands, until the astronomical observations were taken, and then to make a voyage of exploration across the Southern Pacific, of which but little was known. Previous voyages across the Pacific had been made in its middle parts, and, as every ship's crew was attacked by scurvy on a long voyage, it was the commander's chief desire to get across in the shortest time; hence many islands of which we now have knowledge had remained so long undiscovered. But Cook hoped to avoid scurvy by paying much attention to the cleanliness of his ship and crew, and to the variety and quality of their food, and he was very successful, for he suffered less from this disease than any of his predecessors, and since his time scurvy has not been allowed to weaken ships' crews as it previously did.

From very early times there had been a belief in the existence of a Southern Continent, balancing the Northern, but no one had searched for it. The Dutch had acquired possessions and made settlements in the East Indies, and a Dutch navigator, Tasman, had in 1642 found the western coast of what we now know as Australia, and part of the western coast of New Zealand. But he had not determined their southern extremities, and it seemed not impossible that these lands were part of the Southern Continent.

In the ship *Endeavour*, of 370 tons, Cook set sail from Deptford at the end of July, 1768. In the middle of January, 1769, he doubled Cape Horn, and reached Tahiti in April. He spent three months here, making the astronomical observations for which he had come, exploring and surveying the group of islands, and making the acquaintance of the natives, whom he found a happy, simple people, but incorrigible thieves. Leaving the Society Islands early in August, he steered to the south, looking for the supposed Southern Continent. He reached 40° south in stormy weather without finding land, and then turned west. On October 7th he sighted the eastern shore of the North Island of New Zealand, and spent nearly six months surveying the coast-line of the group. He turned north and sailed round the North Island; then passed through the middle strait, to which he gave his own name, spending most of January, 1770, in Queen Charlotte Sound, overhauling the ship, and taking formal possession; then he turned south, and sailed round the South Island, of which he thought Stewart Island a part.

He quitted New Zealand on April 1st, and again sailed west, falling in with the south-east point of Australia on the 19th, but just missing Tasmania. Until nearly the end of August he sailed northwards along two thousand miles of the east coast; surveyed it; gathered information about the people, the plants, and the animals; navigated with great skill the difficult passages of the Great Barrier Reef, where he was nearly wrecked; and took possession of this island-continent for his country.

Cook next sailed through Torres Strait, showing that Australia and New Guinea are not joined; called at the Dutch colony of Batavia, in Java, to overhaul his ship; and then came home by the Cape of Good Hope, reaching the Downs in June, 1771.

One very remarkable feature of this voyage should be noted: the crew was almost free from illness till Batavia was reached, but the shockingly insanitary state of that town led to a most serious outbreak of fever and scurvy, and on the return voyage twenty-three men died.

## 1. THE ISLAND OF MADEIRA

On the 12th of September, 1768, we discovered the islands of Porto Santo and Madeira, and on the next day anchored in Funchal road, and moored with the stream-anchor. When the island of Madeira is first approached from the sea it has a very beautiful appearance. The sides of the hills are entirely covered with vines almost as high as the eye can distinguish, and the vines are green when every kind of herbage, except where they shade the ground, and here and there by the sides of a rill, is entirely burnt up, which was the case at this time.

On the 13th, about eleven o'clock in the forenoon, a boat, which our sailors call the product boat, came on board from the officers of health, without whose permission no person is suffered to land from on board a ship. As soon as this permission was obtained, we went on shore at Funchal, the capital of the island, and proceeded immediately to the house of Mr. Cheap, who is the English consul there, and one of the most considerable merchants of the place. This gentleman received us with the kindness of a brother and the liberality of a prince; he insisted upon our taking possession of his house, in which he furnished us with every possible accommodation during our stay upon the island; he procured leave for Mr. Banks and Dr. Solander to search the island for such mineral curiosities as they should think worth their notice; he employed persons to take fish and gather shells, which time would not permit them to collect for themselves; and he provided horses and guides to take them to any part of the country which they should choose to visit. With all these advantages, however, their excursions were seldom pushed farther than three miles from the town, as they were only five days on shore, one of which they spent at home in receiving the honour of a visit from the governor.

There is great reason to suppose that this whole island was, at some remote period, thrown up by the explosion of subterraneous fire, as every stone, whether whole or in fragments, that we saw upon it appeared to have been burnt, and even the sand itself to be nothing more than ashes. We did not, indeed, see much of the country, but the people informed us that what we did see was a very exact specimen of the rest.

The only article of trade in this island is wine, and the manner in which it is made is very simple. The grapes are put into a square wooden vessel, the dimensions of which are proportioned to the size of the vineyard to which it belongs. The servants then, having taken off their stockings and jackets, get into it, and with their feet and elbows press out as much of the juice as they can. The stalks are afterwards collected, and being tied together with a rope are put under a square piece of wood, which is pressed down upon them by a lever with a stone tied to the end of it. The inhabitants have made so little improvement in knowledge or art, that they have but very lately brought all the fruit of a vineyard to be of one sort by engrafting their vines. It was with great difficulty that they were persuaded to do this, and some of them still obstinately refuse to adopt the practice, though a whole vintage is very often spoiled by the number of bad grapes that are mixed in the vat, but which they will not throw away, because they increase the quantity of the wine.

We saw no wheel-carriages of any sort in the place, which perhaps is not more owing to the want of ingenuity to invent them than to want of industry to mend the roads, which, at present, it is impossible that any wheel-carriage should pass. The inhabitants have horses and mules, indeed, excellently adapted to such ways; but their wine is, notwithstanding, brought to town, from the vine-yards where it is made, in vessels of goatskins, which are carried by men upon their heads. The only imitation of a carriage among this people is a board, made somewhat hollow in the middle, to one end of which a pole is tied by a strap of leather. This wretched sledge approaches about as near to an English cart as an Indian canoe does to a ship's long-boat; and even this would probably never have been thought of if the English had not introduced wine-vessels which are too big to be carried by hand, and which, therefore, are dragged about the town upon these machines.

One reason, probably, why art and industry have done so little for Madeira is that nature has done so much. The soil is very rich, and there is such a difference of climate between the plains and the hills, that there is scarcely a single object of luxury that grows either in Europe or in the Indies that might not be produced here. The hills produce, almost spontaneously, walnuts, chestnuts, and apples in great abundance; and in the town there are many plants that are the natives both of the East and of the West Indies, particularly the banana, the guava, the pine-apple or anana, and the mango, which flourish almost without culture. The corn of this country is of a most excellent quality, large-grained and very fine, and the island would produce it in great plenty; yet most of what is consumed by the inhabitants is imported. The mutton, pork, and beef are also very good; the beef in particular that we took on board was universally allowed to be scarcely inferior to our own; the lean part was very much like it, in both colour and grain, though the beasts are much smaller, but the fat is as white as the fat of mutton.

The churches of Funchal are loaded with ornaments, among which are many pictures and images of the favourite saints; but the pictures are in general wretchedly painted, and the saints are dressed in laced clothes. Some of the convents are in better taste, especially that of the Franciscans, which is plain, simple, and neat in the highest degree. The infirmary in particular drew our attention as a model which might be adopted in other countries with great advantage. It consists of a long room, on one side of which are the windows, and an altar for the convenience of administering the sacrament to the sick; the other side is divided into wards, each of which is just big enough to contain a bed, and neatly lined with tiles. Behind these wards, and parallel to the room in which they stand, there runs a long gallery, with which each ward communicates by a door, so that the sick may be supplied separately with what they want without disturbing their neighbours.

In this convent there is also a singular curiosity of another kind: a small chapel, the whole lining of which, both sides and ceiling, is composed of human skulls and thigh-bones. The thigh-bones are laid across each other, and a skull is placed in each of the four angles.

We visited the good Fathers of this convent on a Thursday evening, just before supper-time, and they received us with great politeness. "We will not ask you", said they, "to sup with us, because we are not prepared; but if you will come to-morrow, though it is a fast with us, we will have a turkey roasted for you." This invitation, which showed a liberality of sentiment not to have been expected in a convent of Portuguese Friars at this place, gratified us much, though it was not in our power to accept it.

We visited also a convent of nuns, dedicated to Santa Clara, and the ladies did us the honour to express a particular pleasure in seeing us there. They had heard that there were great philosophers among us, and, not knowing at all what were the objects of philosophical knowledge, they asked us several questions that were absurd and extravagant in the highest degree. One was, when it would thunder; and another, whether a spring of fresh water was to be found anywhere within the walls of their convent, of which it seems they were in great want. It will naturally be supposed that our answers to such questions were neither satisfactory to the ladies, nor, in their estimation, honourable to us; yet their disappointment did not in the least lessen their civility, and they talked without ceasing during the whole of our visit, which lasted about half an hour.

The hills of this country are very high; the highest, Pico Ruivo, rises 6568 feet, which is much higher than any land that has been measured in Great Britain. The sides of these hills are covered with vines to a certain height, above which are woods of chestnut and pine of immense extent, and above them forests of wild timber of various kinds

not known in Europe, some of which are so
beautiful that they would be a great ornament to
the gardens of Europe.

## 2. THE INHABITANTS OF TIERRA DEL FUEGO

On January 20th, 1769, Mr. Banks and Dr.
Solander went on shore to visit an Indian town,
which some of the people had reported to lie about
two miles up the country. The town was situated
on a dry knoll, or small hill, covered with wood,
none of which seemed to have been cleared away,
and consisted of about twelve or fourteen hovels of
the rudest structure that can be imagined. They
were nothing more than a few poles set up so as to
incline towards each other, and meet at the top,
forming a kind of cone, like some of our bee-hives;
on the weather side they were covered with a few
boughs and a little grass; and on the lee side
about one-eighth of the circle was left open for a
door and a fireplace.

Furniture they had none; a little grass, which
lay round the inside of the hovel, served for both
chairs and beds; and of all the utensils which
necessity and ingenuity have concurred to produce
among other savage nations, they saw only a basket
to carry in the hand, a satchel to hang at the back,
and the bladder of some beast to hold water,

which the natives drink through a hole that is made near the top for that purpose.

The inhabitants of this town were a small tribe, not more than fifty in number. Their colour resembles that of the rust of iron mixed with oil, and they have long black hair. The men are large, but clumsily built; their stature is from five feet eight to five feet ten; the women are much less, few of them being more than five feet high. Their whole apparel consists of the skin of a huanaco or a seal, which is thrown over their shoulders exactly in the state in which it came from the animal's back; a piece of the same skin which is drawn over their feet and gathered round the ankles; and a small piece hanging in front from a waist-belt. The men wear their cloaks open, but the women tie theirs about their waists with a thong.

But although they are content to be naked, they are very ambitious to be fine. Their faces were painted in various forms; the region of the eye was in general white, and the rest of the face adorned with horizontal streaks of red and black; yet scarcely any two were exactly alike. Both men and women wore bracelets of such beads as they could make themselves of small shells and bones; the women both upon their wrists and ankles, the men upon their wrists only. They seemed to set a particular value upon anything that was red, and preferred beads to even a knife or a hatchet.

We saw no appearance of their having any food but shell-fish; for although seals were frequently seen near the shore, they seemed to have no implements for taking them. The shell-fish are collected by the women, whose business it seems to be to attend at low water, with a basket in one hand, a stick, pointed and barbed, in the other, and a satchel at their backs; with the stick they loosen the limpets and other shell-fish that adhere to the rocks, and put them into the basket, which, when full, they empty into the satchel.

The only things that we found among them in which there was the least appearance of neatness or ingenuity were their weapons, which consisted of a bow and arrows. The bow was not inelegantly made, and the arrows were the neatest that we had ever seen; they were of wood, polished to the highest degree, and the point, which was of glass or flint, and barbed, was formed and fitted with wonderful dexterity. We saw also some pieces of glass and flint among them unwrought, besides rings, buttons, cloth, and canvas, with other European commodities; they must, therefore, sometimes travel to the northward, for it is many years since any ship has been so far south as this part of Tierra del Fuego.

### 3. ARRIVAL AT THE SOCIETY ISLANDS

About one o'clock on Monday, the 10th of April, 1769, some of the people who were looking out for the island to which we were bound [Tahiti] said they saw land ahead, in that part of the horizon where it was expected to appear; but it was so faint that whether there was land in sight or not remained a matter of dispute till sunset. The next morning, however, at six o'clock, we were convinced that those who said they had discovered land were not mistaken; it appeared to be very high and mountainous, and we knew it to be the same that had been called King George III's Island.

We were delayed in our approach to it by light airs and calms, so that in the morning of the 12th we were but little nearer than we had been the night before; but about seven a breeze sprang up, and before eleven several canoes were seen making towards the ship. There were but few of them, however, that would come near, and the people in those that did could not be persuaded to come on board. In every canoe there were young plantains, and branches of a tree which the natives called

*E'Midho*; these, as we afterwards learnt, were brought as tokens of peace and amity, and the people in one of the canoes handed them up the ship's side, making signals at the same time with great earnestness, which we did not immediately understand. At length we guessed that they wished that these symbols should be placed in some conspicuous part of the ship; we therefore immediately stuck them among the rigging, at which they expressed the greatest satisfaction. We then purchased their cargoes, consisting of cocoa-nuts and various kinds of fruit, which after our long voyage were very acceptable.

We stood on with an easy sail all night, and about seven o'clock in the morning we came to an anchor in Port-royal Bay, called by the natives *Matavai*. We were immediately surrounded by the natives in their canoes, who gave us cocoa-nuts, fruit resembling apples, bread-fruit, and some small fishes, in exchange for beads and other trifles. They had with them a pig, which they would not part with for anything but a hatchet, and therefore we refused to purchase it; because if we gave them a hatchet for a pig now, we knew they would never afterwards sell one for less, and we could not afford to buy as many as it was probable we should want, at that price.

The bread-fruit grows on a tree that is about the size of a middling oak; its leaves are frequently a foot and a half long, of an oblong shape, deeply sinuated like those of the fig-tree, which they resemble in consistence and colour, and in the exuding of a white milky juice upon being broken. The fruit is about the size and shape of a child's head, and the surface is reticulated not much unlike a truffle; it is covered with a thin skin, and has a core about as big as the handle of a small knife. The eatable part lies between the skin and the core; it is as white as snow, and somewhat of the consistence of new bread; it must be roasted before it is eaten, being first divided into three or four parts; its taste is insipid, with a slight sweet-ness, somewhat resembling that of the crumb of wheaten bread mixed with a Jerusalem artichoke.

As soon as the ship was properly secured I went on shore with Mr. Banks and Dr. Solander, and a party of men under arms. We were received from the boat by some hundreds of the inhabitants, whose looks at least gave us welcome, though they were struck with such awe that the first who approached us crouched so low that he almost crept upon his hands and knees. It is remarkable that he, like the people in the canoes, presented to us the same symbol of peace that is known to have been in use among the ancient and mighty nations of the northern hemisphere, the green branch of a tree. We received it with looks and gestures of kindness and satisfaction, and, observing that each of them held one in his hand, we immediately gathered everyone a bough, and carried it in our hands in the same manner.

During our walk the natives had shaken off their first timid sense of our superiority, and were become familiar; they went with us from the watering-place and took a circuit through the woods. As we went along we distributed beads and other small presents among them, and had the satisfaction to see that they were much gratified.

Our circuit was not less than four or five miles, through groves of trees which were loaded with cocoa-nuts and bread-fruit, and afforded the most grateful shade. Under these trees were the habitations of the people, most of them being only a roof without walls; and the whole scene realized the poetical fables of Arcadia. We remarked, however, not without some regret, that in all our walk we had seen only two hogs, and not a single fowl.

#### 4. THE INHABITANTS OF TAHITI

The people are of the largest size of Europeans. The men are tall, strong, well-limbed, and finely shaped.   The tallest that we saw measured six feet three inches and a half.   The women of the superior rank are also in general above our middle stature, but those of the inferior class are rather below it, and some of them are very small.

Their natural complexion is that kind of clear olive or *brunette* which many people in Europe prefer to the finest white and red.   In those that are exposed to the wind and the sun it is considerably deepened, but in others that live under shelter, especially the superior class of women, it continues of its native hue, and the skin is most delicately smooth and soft; they have no tint in their cheeks which we distinguish by the name of colour.   The shape of the face is comely, the cheek-bones are not high, neither are the eyes hollow, nor the brow prominent; the only feature that does not correspond with our ideas of beauty is the nose, which, in general, is somewhat flat; but their eyes, especially those of the women, are full of expression, sometimes sparkling with fire, and sometimes melting with softness; their teeth also are, almost without exception, most beautifully even and white, and their breath perfectly without taint.

The hair is almost universally black, and rather coarse; the men have beards, which they wear in many fashions, always, however, plucking out great part of them, and keeping the rest perfectly clean and neat.

In their movements there is at once vigour and ease; their walk is graceful, their deportment liberal, and their behaviour to strangers and to each other affable and courteous. In their dispositions also they seemed to be brave, open, and candid, without either suspicion or treachery, cruelty or revenge, so that we placed the same confidence in them as in our best friends.

## 5. TATTOOING

The natives of Tahiti have a custom of staining their bodies nearly in the same manner as is practised in many other parts of the world, which they call tattooing. They prick the skin, so as just not to fetch blood, with a small instrument something in the form of a hoe; that part which answers to the blade is made of a bone or shell, scraped very thin, and is from a quarter of an inch to an inch and a half wide; the edge is cut into sharp teeth or points, from the number of three to twenty, according to its size. When this is to be used, they dip the teeth into a mixture of water and a kind of lamp-black, formed of the smoke that rises from an oily nut that they burn instead of candles; the teeth are then placed upon the skin, and the handle to which they are fastened being struck, by quick smart blows, with a stick fitted to the purpose, they pierce it, and at the same time carry into the puncture the black composition, which leaves an indelible stain.

The operation is painful, and it is some days before the wounds are healed. It is performed upon the youth of both sexes when they are about twelve or fourteen years of age, on several parts of the body, and in various figures, according to the fancy of the parent, or perhaps the rank of the party. The women are generally marked in the form of a Z on every joint of their fingers and toes, and frequently round the outside of their feet; the men are also marked with the same figure, and both men and women have squares, circles, crescents, and ill-designed representations of men, birds, or dogs, and various other devices, impressed upon their legs and arms, some of which we were told had significations, though we could never learn what they were.

But the parts on which these ornaments are lavished with the greatest profusion are the thighs and hips. These, in both sexes, are covered with a deep black, above which arches are drawn one over another as high as the short ribs. They are often a quarter of an inch broad, and the edges are not straight lines, but indented. These arches are their pride, and are shown by men and women with a mixture of ostentation and pleasure, whether as an ornament or as a proof of their fortitude and resolution in bearing pain we could not determine. The face in general is left unmarked.

Mr. Banks saw the operation of tattooing being performed upon a girl about thirteen years old. The instrument used upon this occasion had thirty teeth, and every stroke, of which at least a hundred were made in a minute, drew serum a little tinged with red. The girl bore it with most stoical resolution for about a quarter of an hour; but the pain of so many hundred punctures as she had received in that time then became intolerable; she first complained in murmurs, then wept, and at last burst into loud lamentations, earnestly imploring the operator to desist. He, however, was inexorable; and when she began to struggle she was held down by two women, who sometimes soothed and sometimes chid her, and now and then, when she was most unruly, gave her a smart blow. Mr. Banks stayed in a neighbouring house an hour, and the operation was not over when he went away; yet it was performed but upon one side, the other having been done sometime before; and the arches upon the loins, in which they most pride themselves, and which give more pain than all the rest, were still to be done.

## 6. DRESS IN TAHITI

Their dress consists of cloth or matting of different kinds. The cloth is made of the bark of three different trees—the Chinese paper mulberry, the bread-fruit tree, and a tree that resembles the wild fig-tree of the West Indies.

When the trees are of a proper size they are pulled up and stripped of their branches, and the roots and tops are cut off; the bark of the trunks being then slit up lengthways is easily drawn off, and is carried to some running water, and there placed to soak. When it is sufficiently softened, the women-servants go down to the brook and separate the inner bark from the green outside. Being thus prepared in the afternoon, the pieces are spread out upon plantain leaves in the evening in lengths of about eleven or twelve yards, one by the side of another, till they are about a foot broad, and two or three layers are also laid one upon the other. In the morning, when it is nearly dry, the pieces adhere together, so that the whole may be raised from the ground in one piece. It is then beaten with instruments about a foot long and three inches thick made of a hard wood. The

shape of this instrument is not unlike a square
razor-strop, only that the handle is longer, and
each of its four faces is marked lengthways with
small grooves of different degrees of fineness. They
beat it first with the coarsest side of this mallet;
it spreads very fast under the strokes, chiefly,
however, in the breadth, and the grooves in the
mallet mark it with the appearance of threads; it
is successively beaten with the other sides, last
with the finest, and is then fit for use. The colours
with which they dye this cloth are principally red
and yellow. Of the thin cloth they seldom dye
more than the edges, but the thick cloth is coloured
through the whole surface.

The cloth, which will not bear wetting, they
wear in dry weather, and the matting when it
rains; they are put on in many different ways,
just as their fancy leads them, for in their garments
nothing is cut into shape, nor are any two pieces
sewed together.

The dress of the better sort of women consists
of three or four pieces; one piece, about two yards
wide and eleven yards long, they wrap several
times round their waist, so as to hang down like
a petticoat as low as the middle of the leg; two or
three other pieces, about two yards and a half long
and one wide, each having a hole cut in the middle,

they place one upon another, and then, putting the head through the holes, they bring the long ends down before and behind; they remain open at the sides, and give liberty to the arms; they are gathered round the waist, and confined with a girdle or sash of thinner cloth, which is long enough to go many times round them.

The dress of the men is the same, except that instead of suffering the cloth that is wound round the hips to hang down like a petticoat, they bring it between their legs so as to have some resemblance to breeches.

This is the dress of all ranks of people, and being universally the same as to form, the upper classes distinguish themselves from the lower by the quantity; some of them will wrap round them several pieces of cloth eight or ten yards long and two or three broad, and some throw a large piece loosely over their shoulders in the manner of a cloak, or perhaps two pieces, if they are great personages and are desirous to appear in state.

On their heads the women sometimes wear little turbans, and sometimes a dress which they value much more, and which, indeed, is much more becoming. This consists of human hair plaited in threads scarcely thicker than sewing silk. Mr. Banks has pieces of it above a mile in length

without a knot.   These they wind round the head
in such a manner as produces a very pretty effect,
and in a very great quantity; for I have seen five
or six such pieces wound about the head of one
woman.   Among these threads they stick flowers
of various kinds.   The men sometimes stick the
tail-feather of the Tropic-bird upright in their hair,
which is often tied in a bunch upon the top of their
heads.   Sometimes they wear a kind of garland
made of flowers of various kinds stuck into a
piece of the rind of a plantain, or of scarlet peas
stuck with gum upon a piece of wood; and sometimes they wear a kind of wig made of the hair
of men or dogs, or perhaps of cocoa-nut strings
woven upon one thread, which is tied under their
hair, so that these artificial honours of their head
may hang down behind.   Both sexes wear ear-
rings, but they are placed only on one side.   When
we came they consisted of shell, stone, berries, red
peas, or some small pearls; but our beads very
soon supplanted them all.

## 7. GENERAL ACCOUNT OF NEW ZEALAND

New Zealand was first discovered by Abel Jansen
Tasman, a Dutch navigator, on the 13th of December in the year 1642.   He traversed the western
shore except the most southern part, and entered

the strait which divides the two islands; but being attacked by the natives soon after he came to an anchor, in the place to which he gave the name of Murderer's Bay, he never went on shore. As the whole of this country, except that part of the coast which was seen by Tasman from on board his ship, has from his time to the voyage of the *Endeavour* remained altogether unknown, it has by many been supposed to be part of a southern continent. It is, however, now known to consist of two large islands, divided from each other by a strait or passage, which is about four or five leagues broad. [Cook did not see that "Stewart" Isle is separated from the South Island.]

The southern island is for the most part a mountainous, and, to all appearance, a barren country; and the people whom we saw in Queen Charlotte's Sound, those that came off to us under the snowy mountains and the fires to the west of Cape Saunders, were all the inhabitants and signs of inhabitants that we discovered upon the whole island.

The northern island has a much better appearance; it is indeed not only hilly, but mountainous; yet even the hills and mountains are covered with wood, and every valley has a rivulet of water; the soil in these valleys, and in the plains, of which

there are many that are not overgrown with wood,
is in general light but fertile, and in our opinion
every kind of European grain, plants, and fruit
would flourish here in the utmost luxuriance.
From the vegetation that we found here, there is
reason to conclude that the winters are milder than
those in England, and we found the summer not
hotter, though it was more equally warm; so that
if this country should be settled by people from
Europe, they would, with little industry, be very
soon supplied not only with the necessaries, but
with the luxuries of life in great abundance.

### 8. THE NATIVES OF NEW ZEALAND

The stature of the men in general is equal to the
largest of those in Europe; they are stout, well-
limbed, and fleshy, but not fat like the lazy and
luxurious inhabitants of the islands in the South
Seas.    They are also exceedingly vigorous and
active; and have an adroitness and manual dexterity
in an uncommon degree, which are discovered in
whatever they do.    Their colour in general is
brown, but in few deeper than that of a Spaniard
who has been exposed to the sun, in many not so
deep.    The women have not a feminine delicacy in
their appearance, but their voices are remarkably
soft; and by that, the dress of both sexes being the

same, they are principally distinguished. They have, however, like the women of other countries, more airy cheerfulness and a greater flow of animal spirits than the other sex. Their hair is black, and their teeth extremely regular and as white as ivory; the features of both sexes are good; they seem to enjoy good health, and we saw many who appeared to be of a great age.

The dispositions of both the men and the women seemed to be mild and gentle; they treat each other with the tenderest affection, but are implacable towards their enemies, to whom they never give quarter.

It appears that their principal food is fish, which can be procured only upon the sea-coast, and there in sufficient quantities only at certain times; the tribes, therefore, that live inland, if any such there are, and even those upon the coast, must be frequently in danger of famine. Their country produces neither sheep, nor goats, nor hogs, nor cattle, and of tame fowls they have none. If there are any who are cut off from a supply of fish, their only animal food except dogs, they have nothing to support life but some vegetables, of which the chief are fern-root, yams, and sweet-potatoes. These considerations may enable us to account for the horrid practice of eating those who are killed in battle.

These people, being used to war, and considering every stranger as an enemy, were always disposed to attack us when they were not intimidated by our manifest superiority. At first they had no notion of any superiority but that of numbers; and when this was on their side they considered all our expressions of kindness as the artifices of fear and cunning to circumvent them and preserve ourselves. But when they were once convinced of our power, after having provoked us to the use of our firearms, though loaded with only small-shot, they became at once friendly and even affectionate, placing in us the most unbounded confidence, and doing every-thing that could incite us to put equal confidence in them. It is also remarkable that, when an inter-course was once established between us, they were very rarely detected in any act of dishonesty.

In personal cleanliness they are not equal to our friends of Tahiti, because, not having the advantage of so warm a climate, they do not so often go into the water; but the most disgustful thing about them is the oil with which they anoint their hair. It is certainly the fat either of fish or of birds melted down; and, though the better sort have it fresh, their inferiors use that which is rancid, and consequently are almost as disagreeable to the smell as a Hottentot.

The bodies of both sexes are marked with the black stains called tattooing; but the men are more marked, and the women less. The women in general stain no part of their bodies but the lips, though sometimes they are marked with small black patches on other parts. The men, on the contrary, seem to add something every year to their ornaments, so that some of them, who appeared to be of an advanced age, were almost covered from head to foot. Besides the tattoo-marks they have others, impressed by a method not known to us, of an extraordinary kind; they are furrows of about a line deep and a line broad, such as appear upon the bark of a tree that has been cut through after a year's growth; the edges of these furrows are afterwards indented by the same method, and, being perfectly black, they make a most frightful appearance. The faces of the old men are almost covered with these marks; those who are very young black only their lips like the women; when they are somewhat older they have generally a black patch upon one cheek and over one eye; and so they proceed gradually, that they may grow old and honourable together. The marks upon the face in general are spirals, which are drawn with great nicety, and even elegance, those on one side exactly corresponding with those on the other.

Their dress is made of the leaves of the New Zealand flax. These leaves are split into three or four slips, and the slips, when they are dry, are interwoven with each other into a kind of stuff between netting and cloth, with all the ends, which are eight or nine inches long, hanging out on the upper side. Of this cloth two pieces serve for a complete dress; one of them is tied over their shoulders with a string, and reaches as low as the knees; the other piece is wrapped round the waist, and reaches nearly to the ground; the lower garment, however, is worn by the men only upon particular occasions.

Besides this coarse thatch they have also cloth with a smooth surface, one sort like coarse canvas, and one like cane matting. This is frequently striped, and always has a pretty appearance, as the fibres are so prepared as to shine like silk. To both these they work borders of different colours, of various patterns, and with a neatness and even an elegance which, considering that they have no needle, is surprising. But the great pride of their dress consists in the fur of their dogs, which they cut into stripes, and sew them upon their cloth at a distance from each other. These stripes are also of different colours, and disposed so as to produce a pleasing effect. We saw some dresses that were adorned with feathers instead of fur, but these were not common; and we saw one that was entirely covered with the red feathers of the parrot.

## 9. THE NEW ZEALANDERS WERE CANNIBALS

On January 16th, 1770, some of us went ashore; in our way we saw something floating upon the water which we took for a dead seal, but on rowing up to it found it to be the body of a woman, which to all appearance had been dead some days. We landed, and found a small family of natives, who appeared to be greatly terrified at our approach, and all ran away except one. A conversation between this person and our interpreter soon brought back the rest, except an old man and a child, who still kept aloof, but stood peeping at us from the woods. Our curiosity soon led us to enquire after the body of the woman that we had seen floating upon the water; and they told us that she was a relation who had died a natural death, and that, according to their custom, they had tied a stone to the body and thrown it into the sea, but they supposed the stone had by some accident been disengaged.

This family, when we came on shore, was employed in dressing some provisions; the body of a dog was at this moment in their oven, and many

provision baskets stood near it.   Having cast our
eyes carelessly into one of these as we passed it, we
saw two bones pretty cleanly picked, which did not
seem to be the bones of a dog, and which, upon a
nearer examination, we discovered to be those of
a human body.   At this sight we were struck with
horror, though it was only a confirmation of what
we had heard many times since we arrived upon
this coast.   As we could have no doubt that the
bones were human, neither could we have any
doubt that the flesh which had covered them had
been eaten.   They were found in a provision
basket, the flesh that remained appeared manifestly
to have been dressed by fire, and in the gristles at
the end were the marks of the teeth that had
gnawed them.   To put an end, however, to conjecture founded upon circumstances and appearances, we directed our interpreter to ask what
bones they were; and the natives, without the
least hesitation, answered that they were the bones
of a man; they were then asked what was become
of the flesh, and they replied that they had eaten
it.   "But," said our interpreter, "why did you not
eat the body of the woman which we saw floating
upon the water?"   "The woman", said they, "died
of disease; besides, she was our relation, and we
eat only the bodies of our enemies who are killed

in battle." Upon enquiry who the man was whose bones we had found, they told us that about five days before, a boat belonging to their enemies came into the bay with many persons on board, and that this man was one of seven whom they had killed.

One of us asked whether they had any human bones with the flesh remaining upon them, and upon their answering that all had been eaten, we affected to disbelieve that the bones were human, and said that they were the bones of a dog, upon which one of the natives, with some eagerness, took hold of his own forearm, and thrusting it towards us said that the bone that Mr. Banks held in his hand had belonged to that part of a human body. At the same time, to convince us that the flesh had been eaten, he took hold of his own arm with his teeth, and made show of eating; he also bit and gnawed the bone that Mr. Banks had taken, drawing it through his mouth, and showing by signs that it had afforded a delicious repast. The bone was then returned to Mr. Banks, and he brought it away with him.

## 10. TAKING POSSESSION OF NEW ZEALAND

January 31st, 1770. The carpenter having prepared two posts to be left as memorials of our having visited this place, I ordered them to be inscribed with the king's name, and the year and month; one of them I set up at the watering-place, hoisting the Union flag upon the top of it, and the other I carried over to the island that lies nearest the sea.

I went first to the village, accompanied by Mr. Monkhouse and our interpreter, where I met with our friendly old man, and told him and several others that we were come to set up a mark upon the island, in order to show to any other ship which should happen to come thither that we had been there before. To this they readily consented, and promised that they never would pull it down. I then gave something to everyone present, and to the old man I gave a silver threepence, dated 1736, and some spike nails with the king's broad arrow cut deep upon them, things which I thought most likely to remain long among them.

I then took the post to the highest part of the island, and, after fixing it firmly in the ground, I hoisted upon it the Union flag, and honoured this inlet with the name of Queen Charlotte's Sound, at the same time taking formal possession of this and the adjacent country in the name and for the use of His Majesty King George the Third. We then drank a bottle of wine to Her Majesty's health, and gave the bottle to the old man, who had attended us up the hill, and who was mightily delighted with his present.

## 11. THE NATIVES OF AUSTRALIA AT BOTANY BAY

Having sailed from Cape Farewell of New Zealand on Saturday, the 31st of March, 1770, we sailed westward. On Thursday, the 19th of April, we saw land extending from N.E. to W. at the distance of five or six leagues. We bore away along the shore N.E. for the easternmost land in sight. To the southward no land was to be seen, though it was very clear in that quarter, and the body of Van Diemen's Land ought to have borne due south. As I found this coast trend N.E. and S.W. or rather more to the eastward, I cannot determine whether it joins to Van Diemen's Land or not. [Cook was then at the S.E. corner of Australia, and he sailed northwards along its eastern shore.]

At daybreak on the 28th of April we discovered a bay which seemed to be well sheltered from all winds, and into which therefore I determined to go with the ship. The place where the ship anchored was abreast of a small village of about six or eight houses; and while we were preparing to hoist out the boat, we saw an old woman, followed by three children, come out of the wood; she was loaded

with firewood, and each of the children had also
its little burden.    She often looked at the ship,
but expressed neither fear nor surprise; in a short
time she kindled a fire, and four canoes came in
from fishing.    The men landed, and, having drawn
up their boats, began to dress their dinner, to all
appearance wholly unconcerned about us, though
we were within half a mile of them.    We thought
it remarkable that of all these people we had yet
seen not one had the least appearance of clothing.

We intended to land where we saw the people,
and began to hope that as they had so little re-
garded the ship's coming into the bay, they would
as little regard our coming on shore.    In this,
however, we were disappointed; for as soon as we
approached the rocks, two of the men came down
upon them to dispute our landing, and the rest
ran away.    Each of the two champions was armed
with a lance about ten feet long, and a short stick,
which he seemed to handle as if it was a machine
to assist him in managing or throwing the lance.
They called to us in a very loud tone, and in a
harsh dissonant language, of which neither we nor
our interpreter understood a single word; they
brandished their weapons, and seemed resolved to
defend their coast to the uttermost, though they
were but two and we were forty.

I could not but admire their courage, and, being very unwilling that hostilities should commence, I ordered the boat to lie upon her oars; we then parleyed by signs for a quarter of an hour, and to bespeak their good-will I threw them nails, beads, and other trifles, which they took up and seemed to be very pleased with. I then made signs that I wanted water, and, by all the means that I could devise, endeavoured to convince them that we would do them no harm. They now waved to us, and I was willing to interpret it as an invitation; but on our pulling the boat in they came again to oppose us. One appeared to be a youth of about nineteen or twenty, and the other a man of middle age; as I had now no other resource I fired a musket between them.

Upon the report, the youngest dropped a bundle of lances upon the rock, but, recollecting himself in an instant, he snatched them up again with great haste. A stone was then thrown at us, upon which I ordered a musket to be fired with small shot, which struck the elder upon the legs, and he immediately ran to one of the houses, which was distant about an hundred yards. I now hoped that our contest was over, and we immediately landed; but we had scarcely left the boat when he returned, and we then perceived that he had left the rock only to fetch a shield or target for his defence. As soon as he came up he threw a lance at us, and his comrade another; they fell where we stood thickest, but happily hurt nobody. A third musket with small shot was then fired at them, upon which one of them threw another lance, and both immediately ran away.

We repaired immediately to one of the huts, in one of which we found the children, who had hidden themselves behind a shield and some bark; we peeped at them, but left them in their retreat, without their knowing that they had been discovered, and we threw into the house when we went away some beads, ribbons, pieces of cloth, and other presents, which we hoped would procure us the good-will of the inhabitants when they should return. But the lances which we found lying about we took away with us, to the number of about fifty; they were from six to fifteen feet long, and each of them had four prongs, each of which was pointed with fish-bone and very sharp. Upon examining the canoes that lay upon the beach, we found them to be the worst we had ever seen; they were between twelve and fourteen feet long, and made of the bark of a tree in one piece, which was drawn together and tied up at each end, the middle being kept open by sticks which were placed across them from gunwale to gunwale as thwarts.

The next day, upon visiting the hut where we had seen the children, we were greatly mortified to find that the beads and ribbons which we had left there the night before had not been moved from their place, and that not a native was to be seen.

The great quantity of plants which Mr. Banks and Dr. Solander collected in this place induced me to give it the name of Botany Bay. It is capacious, safe, and convenient. Wood is everywhere plentiful, but I only saw two kinds which may be considered as timber. There are a few shrubs, and several kinds of the palm; mangroves also grow in great plenty near the head of the bay. The country in general is level, and woody, as far as we could see. The woods abound with birds of exquisite beauty, particularly of the parrot kind. About the head of the harbour, where there are large flats of sand and mud, there is great plenty of water-fowl, most of which were altogether unknown to us; one of the most remarkable was black and white, much larger than a swan, and in shape somewhat resembling a pelican.

During my stay in this harbour I caused the English colours to be displayed on shore every day, and the ship's name and the date of the year to be inscribed upon one of the trees near the watering-place.

## 12. THE KANGAROO

Friday, June 22nd, 1770. Some of the people were sent to shoot pigeons, and at their return reported that they had seen an animal as large as a greyhound, of a slender make, a mouse colour, and extremely swift.

June 23rd. This day almost everybody had seen the animal which the pigeon-shooters had brought an account of the day before.

June 24th. As I was walking this morning at a little distance from the ship, I saw myself one of the animals which had been so often described. It was of a light mouse colour, and in size and shape very much resembled a greyhound; it had a long tail also, which it carried like a greyhound; and I should have taken it for a wild dog if, instead of running, it had not leapt like a hare or deer. Its legs were said to be very slender, and the print of its foot to be like that of a goat; but where I saw it the grass was so high that the legs were concealed, and the ground was too hard to receive the track. Mr. Banks also had an imperfect view of this animal, and was of opinon that its species was hitherto unknown.

July 8th. In a walk of many miles some of our men saw four animals of the same kind, two of which Mr. Banks' greyhound fairly chased, but they threw him out at a great distance by leaping over the long thick grass, which prevented his running. These animals were observed not to run upon four legs, but to bound or hop forward upon two.

July 14th. Mr. Gore, who went out this day with his gun, had the good fortune to kill one of the animals which had been so much the subject of our speculation. In form it is most like the jerboa, which it also resembles in its motion, but it greatly differs in size, the jerboa not being larger than a common rat, and this animal, when full grown, being as big as a sheep; this individual was a young one, much under its full growth, weighing only thirty-eight pounds.

The head, neck, and shoulders are very small in proportion to the other parts of the body; the tail is nearly as long as the body, thick near the body, and tapering towards the other end; the fore-legs of this individual were only eight inches long, and the hind-legs two-and-twenty. Its progress is by successive leaps or hops, of a great length, in an erect posture; the fore-legs are kept bent close to the breast, and seemed to be of use only for digging. The skin is covered with a short fur of a dark mouse or gray colour, excepting the head and ears, which bear a slight resemblance to those of a hare.

This animal is called by the natives *Kangaroo*.

The next day our kangaroo was dressed for dinner, and proved most excellent meat. On the 27th Mr. Gore shot a kangaroo which weighed eighty-four pounds. Upon examination, however, we found that this animal was not at its full growth, the innermost grinders not being yet formed. We dressed it for dinner the next day; but, to our great disappointment, we found it had a much worse flavour than that we had eaten before.

### 13. A NARROW ESCAPE FROM SHIPWRECK OFF CAPE TRIBULATION

Hitherto we had safely navigated this dangerous coast, where the sea in all parts conceals shoals that suddenly project from the shore, and rocks that rise abruptly like a pyramid from the bottom, for an extent of two-and-twenty degrees of latitude, more than 1300 miles; and therefore hitherto none of the names that distinguish the several parts of the country that we saw are memorials of distress; but here we became acquainted with misfortune, and we therefore called the point which we had just seen farthest to the northward Cape Tribulation.

This Cape lies in latitude 16° 6′ south, and longitude 145° 21′ east. We steered along the shore N. by W. at the distance of between three and four leagues, having from fourteen to twelve and ten fathom water. On the night of Sunday, June 10th, 1770, a few minutes before eleven, the water shallowed at once from twenty to seventeen fathom, and before the lead could be cast again the ship struck and remained immovable, except by the heaving of the surge that beat her against the crags of the rock upon which she lay. In a few moments everybody was upon the deck, with countenances which sufficiently expressed the horrors of our situation.

We had stood off the shore three hours and a half with a pleasant breeze, and therefore knew that we could not be very near it; and we had too much reason to conclude that we were upon a rock of coral, which is more fatal than any other, because the points of it are sharp, and every part of the surface is so rough as to grind away whatever is rubbed against it even with the gentlest motion.

In this situation all the sails were immediately taken in, and the boats hoisted out to examine the

depth of water round the ship. We soon found
that our fears had not exaggerated our misfortune,
and that the vessel had been lifted over a ledge of
the rock, and lay in a hollow within it; in some
places there was from three to four fathoms, and in
others not so many feet. The ship lay with her
head to the N.E.; and at the distance of about
thirty yards on the starboard side the water
deepened to eight, ten, and twelve fathoms. As
soon as the long-boat was out we struck our yards
and top-masts, and carried out the stream-anchor
on the starboard bow, got the coasting anchor and
cable into the boat, and were going to carry it out
the same way; but on sounding a second time
round the ship, the water was found to be deepest
astern. The anchor therefore was carried out from
the starboard quarter instead of the starboard bow,
that is, from the stern instead of the head; and,
having taken ground, our utmost force was applied
to the capstan, hoping that if the anchor did not
come home the ship would be got off, but to our
great misfortune and disappointment we could not
move her. During all this time she continued to
beat with great violence against the rock, so that
it was with the utmost difficulty that we kept
upon our legs; and, to complete the scene of
distress, we saw by the light of the moon the

sheathing-boards from the bottom of the vessel floating away all round her, and at last her false keel, so that every moment was making way for the sea to rush in that was to swallow us up.

We had now no chance but to lighten her, and we had lost the opportunity of doing that to the greatest advantage, for unhappily we went on shore just at high water, and by this time it had considerably fallen, so that after she should be lightened so as to draw as much less water as the water had sunk, we should be but in the same situation as at first; and the only alleviation of this circumstance was that, as the tide ebbed, the ship settled to the rocks, and was not beaten against them with so much violence. But the rock kept grating her bottom under the starboard bow with such force as to be heard in the fore store-room. That no time might be lost, the water was immediately started in the hold, and pumped up; six of our guns, being all we had upon the deck, our iron and stone ballast, casks, hoop-staves, oil-jars, decayed stores, and many other things that lay in the way of heavier materials were thrown overboard with the utmost expedition. The men were so far impressed with a sense of their situation that not an oath was heard among them, the habit of profaneness, how-

ever strong, being instantly subdued by the dread
of incurring guilt when death seemed to be so near.

At eleven in the forenoon [of the 11th] we
expected high water, and anchors were got out and
everything made ready for another effort to heave
her off if she should float; but to our inexpressible
surprise and concern she did not float by a foot
and a half, though we had lightened her near fifty
tons, so much did the day-tide fall short of that in
the night.   We now proceeded to lighten her still
more, and threw overboard everything that it was
possible for us to spare.

Hitherto she had not admitted much water, but
as the tide fell it rushed in so fast that two pumps,
incessantly worked, could scarcely keep her free.
About five o'clock in the afternoon we observed
the tide begin to rise, but we observed at the same
time that the leak increased to a most alarming
degree, so that two more pumps were manned, but
unhappily only one of them would work.   Three
of the pumps, however, were kept going, and at
nine o'clock the ship righted, but the leak had
gained upon us so considerably that it was
imagined she must go to the bottom as soon as she
ceased to be supported by the rock.   This was a
dreadful circumstance, so that we anticipated the
floating of the ship not as an earnest of deliver-

ance, but as an event that would probably precipi-
tate our destruction, for we well knew that our
boats were not capable of carrying us all on shore.

However, the capstan and windlass were manned
with as many hands as could be spared from the
pumps, and, the ship floating about twenty minutes
after ten o'clock, the effort was made, and she was
heaved into deep water. It was some comfort to
find that she did not now admit more water than
she had done upon the rock; and though, by the
gaining of the leak upon the pumps, there was no
less than three feet nine inches of water in the
hold, yet the men did not relinquish their labour.
But having now endured excessive fatigue of body
and agitation of mind for more than four-and-
twenty hours, and having but little hope of
succeeding at last, they began to flag. None of
them could work at the pump more than five or
six minutes together, and then, being totally
exhausted, they threw themselves down upon the
deck, though a stream of water was running over
it from the pumps between three and four inches
deep.

By eight o'clock the next morning [the 12th]
the pumps had gained considerably upon the leak.
It was, however, impossible to continue this labour,
and as the exact situation of the leak could not be

discovered, we had no hope of stopping it within. In this situation Mr. Monkhouse, one of my midshipmen, came to me and proposed an expedient that he had once seen used on board a merchant vessel. To this man, therefore, the care of the expedient, which is called fothering the ship, was immediately committed, four or five of the people being appointed to assist him; and he performed it in the following manner. He took a lower studding sail, and having mixed together a large quantity of oakum and wool, chopped pretty small, he stitched it down in handfuls upon the sail as lightly as possible, and then plastered it over. When the sail was thus prepared, it was hauled under the ship's bottom by ropes, which kept it extended; and when it came under the leak, the suction which carried in the water carried in with it the oakum and wool from the surface of the sail, which in other parts the water was not sufficiently agitated to wash off. By the success of this expedient our leak was so far reduced that instead of gaining upon three pumps, it was easily kept under with one.

While we lay at anchor for the night we found that the ship made about fifteen inches of water an hour, from which no immediate danger was to be apprehended; and at six o'clock in the morning [the 13th] we weighed and stood to the N.W., edging in for the land. That evening we anchored in four fathoms, at the distance of about two miles from the shore. At nine o'clock one of the mates reported that about two leagues to leeward he had discovered just such a harbour as we wanted, in which there was a sufficient rise of water, and every other convenience that could be desired, either for laying the ship ashore, or heaving her down. [The ship was got into this harbour, thoroughly examined, and repaired.]

At two o'clock in the morning of the 22nd the tide left her, and gave us an opportunity to examine the leak, which we found to be at her floor-heads, a little before the starboard fore-chains. In this place the rocks had made their way through four planks, and even into the timbers. Three more planks were much damaged, and the appearance of these breaches was very extraordinary. There was not a splinter to be seen, but all was as smooth as if the whole had been cut away by an instrument. The timbers in this place were happily very close, and if they had not been so it would have been absolutely impossible to save the ship. But after all, her preservation depended upon a circumstance still more remarkable. One of the holes, which was big enough to have sunk us if we had had eight pumps instead of four, and been able to keep them incessantly going, was in great measure plugged up by a fragment of the rock, which, after having made the wound, was left sticking in it. Upon further examination we found that besides the leak, considerable damage had been done to the bottom; great part of the sheathing was gone from under the larboard bow, and a considerable part of the false keel was also wanting.

## 14. GENERAL ACCOUNT OF AUSTRALIA

New Holland, or, as I have now called the eastern coast, New South Wales, is of a larger extent than any other country in the known world that does not bear the name of a continent. The length of coast along which we sailed amounts to near 2000 miles, so that its surface must be much more than equal to all Europe.

The country is upon the whole rather barren than fertile, yet the rising ground is chequered by woods and lawns, and the plains and valleys are in many places covered with herbage. The grass in general is high but thin, and the trees, where they are largest, are seldom less than forty feet asunder; nor is the country inland, as far as we could examine it, better clothed than the sea-coast. The northern part of the coast abounds with fine bays and harbours, where vessels may lie in perfect security from all winds.

If we may judge by the appearance of the country while we were there, which was in the very height of the dry season, it is very well watered; we found innumerable small brooks and springs, but no great rivers.

Of trees there is no great variety. Of those that could be called timber there are but two sorts; the largest is the gum-tree, which grows all over the country; it has narrow leaves, not much unlike a willow, and the gum, or rather resin, that it yields is of a deep-red colour. The other timber tree grows somewhat like our pines. The wood of both these trees is extremely hard and heavy. Here is a great variety of plants to enrich the collection of a botanist, but very few of them are of the esculent kind.

The number of inhabitants in this country appears to be very small in proportion to its extent. We never saw so many as thirty of them together but once, and that was at Botany Bay. The only tribe with which we had any intercourse consisted of one-and-twenty persons, twelve men, seven women, one boy, and one girl; the women we never saw but at a distance, for when the men came over the river they were left behind.

The men here and in other places were of a middle size, and in general well-made, clean-limbed, and remarkably vigorous, active, and nimble; their countenances were not altogether without expression, and their voices were remarkably soft and effeminate.

Their skins were so uniformly covered with dirt that it was difficult to ascertain their true colour; we made several attempts, by wetting our fingers and rubbing them, to remove the incrustations, but with very little effect. With the dirt they appear nearly as black as a negro; and according to our best discoveries the skin itself is of the colour of wood soot, or what is generally called a chocolate colour. Their features are far from disagreeable, their noses are not flat, nor are their lips thick; their teeth are white and even, and their hair naturally long and black, but universally cropped short; in general it is straight, but sometimes it has a slight curl; we saw none that was not matted and filthy, though without oil or grease. Their beards were of the same colour as their hair, and bushy and thick; they are not, however, suffered to grow long.

Both sexes go stark naked. Their principal ornament is a bone which they thrust through the cartilage that divides the nostrils from each other.

As this bone is as thick as a man's finger, and between five and six inches long, it reaches quite across the face, and so effectually stops up both the nostrils that they are forced to keep their mouths open for breath, and snuffle so when they speak that they are scarcely intelligible even to each other. Besides this nose-jewel they had necklaces made of shells, very neatly cut and strung together; bracelets of small cord, wound two or three times about the upper part of their arm; and a string of plaited human hair, about as thick as a thread of yarn, tied round the waist.

But though these people wear no clothes, their bodies have a covering besides the dirt, for they paint them both white and red. The red is commonly laid on in broad patches upon the shoulders and breast; the white in stripes, some narrow and some broad; the narrow were drawn over the limbs, and the broad over the body, not without some degree of taste. The white was also laid on in small patches upon the face, and drawn in a circle round each eye.

They produce fire with great facility, and spread it in a wonderful manner. To produce it they take two pieces of dry soft wood, one a stick about eight or nine inches long, and the other a flat piece; the stick they shape into an obtuse point at one end, and pressing it upon the other, turn it nimbly by holding it between both their hands, often shifting their hands up, and then moving them down upon it to increase the pressure as much as possible. By this method they get fire in less than two minutes, and from the smallest spark they increase it with great speed and dexterity. We have often seen one of them run along the shore, to all appearance with nothing in his hand, who, stooping down for a moment at the distance of every fifty or a hundred yards, left fire behind him, as we could see by the smoke and then by the flame among the driftwood and other litter that was scattered along the place. We had the curiosity to examine one of these planters of fire when he set off, and we saw him wrap up a small spark in dry grass, which, when he had run a little way, having been fanned by the air that his motion produced, began to blaze; he then laid it down in a place convenient for his purpose, enclosing a spark of it in another quantity of grass, and so continued his course.

### 15. TAKING POSSESSION OF AUSTRALIA

[August 21st, 1770, off Cape York.]

At four o'clock in the afternoon we anchored, being about a mile and a half or two miles within the entrance; the channel here had begun to widen, and the islands on each side of us were distant about a mile; the mainland stretched away to the south-west. Between the mainland and the islands we could see no land, so that we conceived hopes of having at last found a passage into the Indian Sea; however, that I might be able to determine with more certainty, I resolved to land upon the island which lies at the south-east point of the passage.

We climbed the highest hill in the island, which was not more than three times as high as the mast-head, and the most barren of any we had seen. From this hill no land could be seen between the s.w. and w.s.w., so that I had no doubt of finding a passage through. The land to the north-west of it consisted of a great number of islands of various extent and different heights, ranged one behind the other as far to the north-ward and westward as I could see, which could not be less than thirteen leagues.

As I was now about to quit the eastern coast of New Holland, which I had coasted from latitude 38° to this place, and which I am sure no European had ever seen before, I once more hoisted English colours, and though I had already taken possession of several particulars, I now took

possession of the whole eastern coast from latitude
$38°$ to this place, latitude $10\frac{1}{2}°$ s., in right of His
Majesty King George the Third, by the name of
New South Wales, with all the bays, harbours,
rivers, and islands. We then fired three volleys
of small-arms, which were answered by the same
number from the ship. Having performed this
ceremony upon the island, which we called Possession Island, we re-embarked in our boat and
returned to the vessel.

## 16. "RUNNING AMOK" IN JAVA

The Malays are the people among whom the
practice that is called "running amok" has prevailed from time immemorial. It is well known that
to "run amok", in the original sense of the word,
is to get intoxicated with opium, and then to rush
into the street with a drawn weapon, and kill whoever comes in the way, till the person himself is
either killed or taken prisoner. Of this several
instances happened while we were at Batavia; and
one of the officers whose business it is, among other
things, to apprehend such people told us that
there was scarcely a week in which he or some of
his brethren were not called upon to take one of
them into custody.

In one of the instances that came to our knowledge, the man was mad with jealousy before he made himself drunk with opium; and we were told that the native who "runs amok" is always first driven to desperation by some outrage, and always first revenges himself upon those who have done him wrong. We were also told that though these unhappy wretches afterwards run into the street with a weapon in their hand, frantic and foaming at the mouth, yet they never kill any but those who attempt to apprehend them, or those whom they suspect of such an intention, and that whosoever gives them way is safe.

They are generally slaves, who, indeed, are most subject to insults, and least able to obtain legal redress; freemen, however, are sometimes provoked into this extravagance; and one of the persons who "ran amok" while we were at Batavia was free and in easy circumstances. He was jealous of his own brother, whom he first killed, and afterwards he killed two others who attempted to oppose him; he did not, however, come out of his house, but endeavoured to defend himself in it, though the opium had so far deprived him of his senses that of three muskets that he attempted to use against the officers of justice not one was either loaded or primed.

If the officer takes one of these "amoks" alive,

his reward is very considerable, but if he kills them, nothing is added to his pay.   Yet such is the fury of their desperation that three out of four are of necessity destroyed in the attempt to secure them, though the officers are provided with instruments like large tongs or pincers, to lay hold of them without coming within the reach of their weapons.   Those who happen to be taken alive are generally wounded, but they are always broken alive upon the wheel, and if the physician who is appointed to examine their wounds thinks them likely to be mortal, the punishment is inflicted immediately, and the place of execution is generally the spot where the first murder was committed.

## 17. THE CHINESE IN BATAVIA

The Chinese are numerous in this place, but possess very little property; many of them live within the walls, and keep shops.   The street called Passar Pissang, which lies north from the great church and very near it, is inhabited by none but Chinese fruit-sellers, who are supplied from the gardens of gentlemen in the neighbourhood of the town with such as is fresh and excellent of its kind. Others have a rich show of European and Chinese goods.   The greater part, however, live in a quarter by themselves, without the walls, called Campang

China. Many of them are carpenters, joiners, smiths, tailors, slipper-makers, dyers of cotton, and embroiderers, maintaining the character of industry that is universally given of them; and some are scattered about the country, where they cultivate gardens, sow rice and sugar, or keep cattle and buffaloes, whose milk they bring daily to town.

There is nothing, clean or dirty, honest or dishonest, provided there is not too much danger of a halter, that the Chinese will not readily do for money. But though they work with great diligence, and patiently undergo any degree of labour, yet no sooner have they laid down their tools than they begin to game, either at cards or at dice, or some other among the multitude that they have invented, which are altogether unknown in Europe; to this they apply with such eagerness as scarcely to allow time for the necessary refreshments of food and sleep, so that it is as rare to see a Chinese idle as to see a Dutchman or a native employed.

In manners they are always civil, or rather obsequious; and in dress they are remarkably neat and clean, to whatever rank of life they belong. In eating they are easily satisfied, though the few that are rich have many savoury dishes. Rice, with a small proportion of flesh or fish, is the food of the poor; and they have the advantage of the Mahometan natives, whose religion forbids them to eat of many things which they could most easily procure. The Chinese, on the contrary, being under no restraint, eat pork, dogs, cats, frogs, lizards, serpents of many kinds, and a great variety of sea animals which the other inhabitants of this country do not consider as food; they also eat many vegetables which a European, unless he was perishing with hunger, would never touch.

The Chinese have a singular superstition with regard to the burial of their dead; for they will upon no occasion open the ground a second time where a body has been interred. Their burying-grounds, therefore, cover many hundred acres, and the Dutch, grudging the waste of so much ground, will not sell any for this purpose but at the most exorbitant price. They take an uncommon method to preserve the body entire, and to prevent the remains of it from being mixed with the earth that surrounds it. They enclose it in a large thick coffin of wood, not made of planks joined together, but hollowed out of the solid timber like a canoe; this being covered, and let down into the grave, is surrounded with a coat of their mortar about eight or ten inches thick, which in a short time becomes as hard as a stone.

## 18. CAPE TOWN

The Cape of Good Hope has been so often described, and is so well known in Europe, that I
shall mention only a few particulars which in other
relations are omitted or misrepresented.

Notwithstanding all that has been said to the
contrary, no country that we saw during the
voyage makes a more forlorn appearance, or is
in reality a more sterile desert. The land over
the Cape, which constitutes the peninsula formed
by Table Bay on the north and False Bay on
the south, consists of high mountains, altogether
naked and desolate; the land behind these to the
east, which may be considered as the isthmus,
is a plain of vast extent, consisting almost wholly
of a light kind of sea-sand, which produces nothing
but heath, and is utterly incapable of cultivation.
All the spots that will admit of improvement,
which together bear about the proportion to the
whole of one to a thousand, are laid out in vine-
yards, orchards, and kitchen-grounds; and most
of these little spots lie at a considerable distance
from each other. There is also reason to believe
that in the interior parts of the country that
which is capable of cultivation does not bear a
greater proportion to that which is incorrigibly

barren; for the Dutch told us that they had settlements eight-and-twenty days' journey up the country, a distance equal to at least nine hundred miles, from which they bring provisions to the Cape by land; so that it seems reasonable to conclude that provisions are not to be had within a less compass. While we were at the Cape, a farmer came thither from the country, a distance of fifteen days' journey, and brought his young children with him. We were surprised at this, and asked him if it would not have been better to leave them with his next neighbour. "Neighbour!" said the man, "I have no neighbour within less than five days' journey of me." Surely the country must be deplorably barren in which those who settle only to raise provisions for a market are dispersed at such distances from each other.

That the country is everywhere destitute of wood appears to demonstration; for timber and planks are imported from Batavia, and fuel is almost as dear as food. We saw no tree, except in plantations near the town, that was six feet high; and the stems, which were not thicker than a man's thumb, had roots as thick as an arm or a leg, such is the influence of the winds here to the disadvantage of vegetation, setting the sterility of the soil out of the question.

The only town that the Dutch have built here is,

from its situation, called Cape Town, and consists
of about a thousand houses, neatly built of brick,
and whited on the outsides. They are, however,
covered only with thatch, for the violence of the
south-east winds would render any other roof in-
convenient and dangerous. The streets are broad
and commodious, all crossing each other at right
angles. In the principal street there is a canal, on
each side of which is planted a row of oaks, that
have flourished pretty well, and yield an agreeable
shade. There is a canal also in one other part of
the town, but the slope of the ground in the course
of each is so great that they are furnished with
flood-gates or locks at intervals of little more than
fifty yards.

The women in general are very handsome; they
have fine clear skins, and a bloom of colour that
indicates a purity of constitution and high health.
They make the best wives in the world, both as
mistresses of a family and as mothers, and there is
scarcely a house that does not swarm with children.

The air is salutary in a high degree; so that those
who bring diseases hither from Europe generally
recover perfect health in a short time; but the
diseases that are brought from India are not so
certainly cured.

Notwithstanding the natural sterility of the

climate, industry has supplied this place with all the necessaries and even the luxuries of life in the greatest profusion. The beef and mutton are excellent, though the sheep and cattle are natives of the country. The cattle are lighter than ours, more neatly made, and have horns that spread to a much wider extent. The sheep are clothed with a substance between wool and hair, and have tails of an enormous size; we saw some that weighed twelve pounds, and were told that there were many much larger. Good butter is made of the milk of the cows, but the cheese is very much inferior to our own. Here are goats, but they are never eaten, hogs, and a variety of poultry. Hares are also found here, exactly like those of Europe, antelopes of many kinds, quails of two sorts, and bustards which are well-flavoured but not juicy.

The fields produce European wheat and barley, and the gardens European vegetables and fruit of all kinds, besides plantains, guavas, jambu [an East Indian fruit, acid and cooling], and some other Indian fruits; but these are not in perfection, the plantains in particular are very bad, and the guavas no larger than gooseberries. The vineyards also produce wine of various sorts, but not equal to those of Europe, except the Constantia, which is made genuine only at one vineyard about ten miles distant from the town. There is another vineyard near it where wine is made that is called by the same name, but it is greatly inferior.

At the farther end of the High Street, the Company has a garden, which is about two-thirds of an English mile long; the whole is divided by walks that intersect each other at right angles, and are planted with oaks that are clipped into wall-hedges, except in the centre walk, where they are suffered to grow to their full size, and afford an agreeable shade, which is the more welcome, as, except the plantations by the sides of the two canals, there is not a single tree that would serve even for a shepherd's bush, within many miles of the town.

At the farther end of the garden is a menagerie, in which there are many birds and beasts that are never seen in Europe, particularly a beast called by the Hottentots *Koodoo*, which is as large as a horse, and has the fine spiral horns that are sometimes seen in private and public collections of curiosities.

## THE SECOND VOYAGE, 1772-1775

The great success that had attended Cook's first voyage of circumnavigation aroused much interest in geographical matters, and, among other problems, that of the Southern Continent was more specially discussed.   The belief in a habitable and inhabited Southern Continent had only the slenderest foundation in ascertained fact, but it had been strongly reasserted in geographical publications just before Cook's return, and the discoveries he had made of the insularity of New Zealand and the probable insularity of "New Holland" only rendered it necessary to place the "Southern Continent" somewhat farther south than had been previously done.   It was determined to send out an expedition that should clear up this matter, and Cook was placed in command of two ships, the *Resolution*, of 462 tons, and the *Adventure*, of 336 tons, the latter under Captain Furneaux.

The ships left Plymouth on July 13th, 1772, and sailed for Cape Town, which was reached at the end of October.   Then in the summer of the southern hemisphere they sailed to the south; on January 17th, 1773, they were within the Antarctic Circle, but were stopped by the ice; keeping mainly near the parallel of 60° south, they sailed to the east, seeing much ice and fog, but no "Southern Continent".   Early in February, in the fog the ships got parted, but each sailed past the south of Australia, thus showing it to be no part of the "Southern Continent", and the *Adventure* touched at Tasmania, but without finding that it was a separate island.   The ships met in Queen Charlotte Sound of New Zealand in the middle of May.

In June they started for the Mid-Pacific, to spend the southern winter in a cruise among the islands.   They reached

Tahiti in the middle of August, and left it in the middle of September, visiting the Friendly Isles toward the end of that month, and going on to New Zealand again at the end of October. Here they satisfied themselves that the New Zealanders were cannibals. The *Adventure* parted company when they reached New Zealand, and was not seen again during the voyage. While she was in Queen Charlotte Sound some of her men were killed and eaten by the New Zealanders. She returned to England in July, 1774.

During the southern summer of 1773–74 Cook sailed east through the southern ocean between the longitudes of New Zealand and South America, twice passing within the Antarctic Circle, and reaching a higher south latitude than anyone had previously reached. Judging that there was nothing but ice or ice-covered land to the south, he turned north to Easter Isle, noting its curious sculptures, and then returned to New Zealand, on the way visiting again the Marquesas, Society, and Friendly Islands, exploring the New Hebrides, and discovering New Caledonia.

He remained at Queen Charlotte Sound from October 18th to November 10th, overhauling and repairing his ship, and preparing for the return voyage. Passing Cape Horn on December 29th, he bore away to the south-east in search for possible lands, and South Georgia was discovered, and taken formal possession of, in the middle of January, 1775. At Cape Town they remained for repairs from March 22nd to April 27th, and then came home, reaching Portsmouth on July 30th.

For this remarkable voyage the official reward Cook received was an appointment to a Captaincy in Greenwich Hospital, which meant practically a retiring allowance. His account of his sanitary treatment for the prevention of scurvy earned for him the Gold Medal of the Royal Society, of which he was elected a Fellow.

## 1. THE SOUTHERN ICE IN 1772-73

December 10th, 1772. At eight o'clock we saw an island of ice to the westward of us, we being then 50° 40′ south, and 2° east of the Cape of Good Hope. The weather coming hazy, I called the *Adventure* by signal under my stern, which was no sooner done than the haze increased so much, with snow and sleet, that we did not see an island of ice, which we were steering directly for, till we were less than a mile from it. I judged it to be about fifty feet high and half a mile in circuit. It was flat at top, and its sides rose in a vertical direction, against which the sea broke exceedingly high. Captain Furneaux at first took this ice for land, and hauled off from it, until called back by signal. As the weather was foggy, it was necessary to proceed with caution. We kept on to the south-ward with the wind at north till night, which we spent in making short trips, first one way and then another, under an easy sail.

December 11th. At daylight in the morning we made sail to the southward, with the wind at west, having a fresh gale, attended with sleet and snow. At noon we saw some white birds about the size of pigeons, with blackish bills and feet. I never saw any such before; and our naturalists had no knowledge of them. I believe them to be of the petrel tribe, and natives of these icy seas. At this time we passed between two ice islands, which lay at a little distance from each other.

December 12th. We still had thick hazy weather, with sleet and snow; so that we were obliged to proceed with great caution on account of the ice islands. Six of these we passed this day, some of them near two miles in circuit and sixty feet high. And yet, such was the force and height of the waves that the sea broke quite over them. This exhibited a view which for a few moments was pleasing to the eye; but when we reflected on the danger, the mind was filled with horror. For were a ship to get against the weather-side of one of these islands when the sea runs high, she would be dashed to pieces in a moment. Upon our getting among the ice islands the albatrosses left us; nor did our other bird companions appear in such numbers; but, on the other hand, penguins began to make their appearance. Two of these birds were seen to-day.

December 13th. The wind in the night became a fresh gale, with sleet and snow, which froze on our sails and rigging as it fell, so that they were all hung with icicles. We kept on to the south-ward, passed no less than eighteen ice islands, and

saw more penguins. At noon we were in the latitude of 54° south. We stood on to the s.s.e. till
eight o'clock in the evening, the weather still continuing thick and hazy, with sleet and snow. From noon
to this time, twenty ice islands of various extent,
both for height and circuit, presented themselves
to our view.

December 14th. At half an hour past six in the
morning we were stopped by an immense field of
low ice, to which we could see no end, to either the
east, west, or south. In different parts of this field
were islands or hills of ice, like those we found floating in the sea; and some on board thought they saw
land also over the ice. I even thought so myself;
but changed my opinion upon more narrowly examining these ice hills, and the various appearances
they made when seen through the haze. For at
this time it was both hazy and cloudy in the horizon, so that a distant object could not be seen
distinctly. We bore away along the edge of the
ice, steering s.s.e. and s.e. according to the direction
of the north side of it, where we saw many whales,
and penguins and other birds.

December 18th. We were now enabled to get
clear of the field of ice; but at the same time we
were carried in amongst the ice islands in a manner
equally dangerous, and which with much difficulty

we kept clear of. Dangerous as it is to fall among these floating rocks (if I may be allowed to call them so) in a thick fog, this, however, is preferable to being entangled with immense fields of ice under the same circumstances. The great danger to be apprehended in this latter case is the getting fast in the ice, a situation which would be exceedingly alarming. I had two men on board that had been in the Greenland trade, the one of them in a ship that lay nine weeks, and the other in one that lay six weeks fast in this kind of ice, which they called packed-ice. What they call field-ice is thicker, and the whole field, be it ever so large, consists of one piece. Whereas this, which I call field-ice, from its immense extent, consists of many pieces of various sizes, both in thickness and in surface, packed close together, and in places heaped one upon another. This, I am of opinion, would be found too hard for a ship's side that is not properly armed against it. How long it may have lain, or will lie here, is a point not easily determined. Such ice is found in the Greenland seas all the summer long, and I think it cannot be colder there in the summer than it is here. Be this as it may, we certainly had no thaw; on the contrary, the mercury kept generally below the freezing point, although it was the middle of summer.

January 4th, 1773. We had the advantage of a fresh gale, and the disadvantage of a thick fog, and much snow and sleet, which, as usual, froze on our rigging as it fell, so that every rope was covered with the finest transparent ice I ever saw. This afforded an agreeable enough sight to the eye, but conveyed to the mind an idea of coldness much greater than it really was; for the weather was rather milder than it had been for some time past, and the sea less encumbered with ice. But the worst was that the ice so clogged the rigging, sails, and blocks, as to make them exceedingly bad to handle. Our people, however, surmounted those difficulties with a steady perseverance, and withstood the cold much better than I expected.

January 8th. At nine o'clock in the evening we came to an ice island that had a quantity of loose ice about it. As the wind was moderate and the weather tolerably fair, we shortened sail and stood on and off, with a view to taking some on board on the return of light. But, at four o'clock in the morning of the 9th, finding ourselves to leeward of this ice, we bore down to an island to leeward of us, there being about it some loose ice, part of which we saw break off. There we brought to, hoisted out three boats, and in about five or six hours took up as much ice as yielded fifteen tons of good fresh water. The pieces we took up were hard and solid as a rock; some of them were so large that we were obliged to break them with pickaxes before they could be taken into the boats. The salt water which adhered to the ice was so trifling as not to be tasted, and, after it had lain on deck a short time, entirely drained off; and the water that the ice yielded was perfectly sweet and well-tasted. Part of the ice we broke in pieces and put into casks; some we melted in the coppers, and filled up the casks with the water; and some we kept on deck for present use. The melting and stowing away of the ice is a little tedious, and takes up some time; otherwise this is the most expeditious way of watering I ever met with.

Five tolerably fine days now succeeded one another. This, besides giving us an opportunity to make some astronomical observations, was very serviceable to us on many other accounts, and came at a very seasonable time. For, having on board a good quantity of fresh water, or ice, which was the same thing, the people were enabled to wash and dry their clothes and linen, a care that can never be enough attended to in all long voyages.

As we met with little ice on the 16th I stood to the south close-hauled. On the 17th, as the wind remained invariably fixed at east, and E. by S., I continued to stand to the south; and between eleven and twelve o'clock we crossed the Antarctic Circle in the longitude of 39° 35' east; for at noon we were by observation in the latitude of 66° 36' 30" south.  The weather was now become tolerably clear, so that we could see several leagues round us, and yet we had seen only one island of ice since the morning.  But about 4 p.m., as we were steering to the south, we observed the whole sea in a manner covered with ice, from the direction of S.E. round by the south to west.

In this space thirty-eight ice islands, great and small, were seen, besides loose ice in abundance, so that we were obliged to luff for one piece and bear up for another; as we continued to advance to the south, it increased in such a manner that, at three-quarters past six, being then in the latitude of 67° 15' south, we could proceed no farther, the ice being entirely closed to the south, in the whole extent from east to w.s.w., without the least appearance of any opening.  This immense field was composed of different kinds of ice, such as high hills, loose or broken pieces packed close together, and what I think Greenlandmen call field-ice.  A float of this kind of ice lay to the S.E. of us, of such extent that I could see no end to it from the mast-head. It was sixteen or eighteen feet high at least, and appeared of a pretty equal height and surface.

After meeting with this ice, I did not think it was at all prudent to persevere in getting farther to the south, especially as the summer was already half spent, and it would have taken up some time to get round the ice, even supposing it to have been practicable, which, however, is doubtful. As the wind still continued at E. by S. I was obliged to return to the north.

February 16th. The wind blew a gentle gale, with which we stood to the southward, having frequent showers of sleet and snow. But in the night we had fair weather and a clear, serene sky; and, between midnight and three o'clock in the morning of the 17th, lights were seen in the heavens, similar to those in the northern hemisphere known by the name of Aurora Borealis or Northern Lights; but I never heard of the Aurora Australis being seen before. The officer of the watch observed that it sometimes broke out in spiral rays and in a circular form; then its light was very strong, and its appearance beautiful. He could not perceive that it had any particular direction; for it appeared, at various times, in different parts of the heavens, and diffused its light throughout the whole atmosphere.

## 2. WATER-SPOUTS NEAR NEW ZEALAND

I directed my course along shore for Queen Charlotte's Sound, where I expected to find the *Adventure*. In this passage we met with nothing remarkable or worthy of notice till May 17th, at four o'clock in the afternoon. Being then about three leagues to the westward of Cape Stephens, having a gentle gale at w. by s., and clear weather, the wind at once flattened to a calm, the sky became suddenly obscured by dark dense clouds, and seemed to forebode much wind. This occasioned us to clew up all our sails, and presently after six water-spouts were seen. Four rose and spent themselves between us and the land, that is, to the s.w. of us; the fifth was without us; the sixth first appeared in the s.w. at the distance of two or three miles at least from us. Its progressive motion was to the N.E., not in a straight but in a crooked line, and it passed within fifty yards of our stern without our feeling any of its effects.

The diameter of the base of this spout I judged to be about fifty or sixty feet; that is, the sea within this space was much agitated, and foamed up to a great height. From this a tube or round body was formed, by which the water or air or both was carried in a spiral stream up to the clouds. Some of our people said they saw a bird in the one near us, which was whirled round like the fly of a jack as it was carried upwards. During the time these spouts lasted we had, now and then, light puffs of wind from all points of the compass, with some few slight showers of rain, which generally fell in large drops, and the weather continued thick and hazy for some hours afterwards, with light variable breezes of wind.

Some of these spouts appeared at times to be stationary, and at other times to have a quick but very unequal progressive motion, and always in a crooked line, sometimes one way and sometimes another, so that once or twice we observed them to cross each other. From the ascending motion of the bird, and several other circumstances, it was very plain to us that these spouts were caused by whirlwinds, and that the water in them was violently hurried upwards, and did not descend from the clouds, as I have heard some assert. The first appearance of them is by the violent agitation and rising up of the water; and presently after you see a round column or tube forming from the clouds above, which apparently descends till it joins the agitated water below. I say apparently, because I believe it not to be so in reality, but that the tube is already formed from the agitated water below, and ascends, though at first it is either too small

or too thin to be seen.   When the tube is formed
or becomes visible, its apparent diameter increases
until it is pretty large; after that it decreases;
and at last it breaks or becomes invisible towards
the lower part.   Soon after, the sea below resumes
its natural state, and the tube is drawn, by little
and little, up to the clouds, where it is dissipated.
The same tube would sometimes have a vertical,
and sometimes a crooked or inclined direction.   I
have been told that the firing of a gun will dissi-
pate them; and I am very sorry that I did not try
the experiment, as we were near enough, and had
a gun ready for the purpose; but as soon as the
danger was past, I thought no more about it,
being too attentive in viewing these extraordinary
meteors.

### 3. HUMAN SACRIFICES IN TAHITI

As I had some reason to believe that amongst their
religious customs human sacrifices were sometimes
considered necessary, I went one day to a *Marai*
[burying-ground] in Matavai in company with
Captain Furneaux, having with us, as I had upon
all other occasions, one of my men who spoke their
language tolerably well, and several of the natives,
one of whom appeared to be an intelligent, sensible
man.   In the *Marai* was a *Tupapow* [a raised

platform with a light roof over it], on which lay a corpse and some viands; so that everything promised success to my enquiries. I began with asking questions relating to the several objects before me, if the plantains, &c., were for the *Eatua* [the God]; if they sacrificed to the *Eatua* hogs, dogs, fowls, &c., to all of which he answered in the affirmative. I then asked if they sacrificed men to the *Eatua*; he answered *Taata eno*, that is, bad men they did, first *Tiparrahy*, or beating them till they were dead. I then asked him if good men were put to death in this manner; his answer was, " No, only *Taata eno*." I next asked him if *Towtows*, that is servants or slaves, who had no hogs, dogs, or fowls, but yet were good men, were sacrificed to the *Eatua*. His answer was, " No, only bad men." I asked him several more questions, and all his answers seemed to tend to this one point, that men for certain crimes were condemned to be sacrificed to the gods, provided they had not wherewithal to redeem themselves. This, I think, implies that on some occasions human sacrifices are considered as necessary, particularly when they take such men as have, by the laws of the country, forfeited their lives and have nothing to redeem them; and such will generally be found among the lower class of people.

### 4. CANNIBALISM IN NEW ZEALAND

On November 23rd, 1773, in the afternoon some of the officers went on shore to amuse themselves among the natives, where they saw the head and bowels of a youth who had lately been killed, lying on the beach, and the heart stuck on a forked stick, which was fixed to the head of one of the largest canoes. One of the gentlemen bought the head and brought it on board, where a piece of the flesh was broiled and eaten by one of the natives, before all the officers and most of the men. I was on shore at this time, but soon after returning on board was informed of the above circumstances; and found the quarter-deck crowded with the natives, and the mangled head, or rather part of it (for the under jaw and lip were wanting), lying on the tafferel. The skull had been broken on the left side just above the temple, and the remains of the face had all the appearance of a youth under twenty.

The sight of the head and the relation of the above circumstances struck me with horror, and filled my mind with indignation against these cannibals. Curiosity, however, got the better of my indignation, especially when I considered that it would avail but little, and, being desirous of becoming an eye-witness of a fact which many doubted, I ordered a piece of the flesh to be broiled and brought to the quarter-deck, where one of these cannibals ate it with surprising avidity. This had such an effect on some of our people as to make them sick.

That the New Zealanders are cannibals can now no longer be doubted. The account given of this in my former voyage, being partly founded on circumstances, was, as I afterwards understood, discredited by many persons. Few consider what a savage man is in his natural state, and even after he is in some degree civilized. The New Zealanders are certainly in some state of civilization; their behaviour to us was manly and mild, showing, on all occasions, a readiness to oblige. They have some arts among them which they execute with great judgment and unwearied patience; they are far less addicted to thieving than the other islanders of the South Sea; and I believe those in the same tribe, or such as are at peace with one another, are strictly honest among themselves. This custom of eating their enemies slain in battle,—and I firmly believe they eat the flesh of no other,—has, undoubtedly, been handed down to them from the earliest times; and we know it is not an easy matter to wean a nation from their ancient customs, let them be ever so inhuman and savage, especially if that nation has no manner of connection or commerce with strangers. For it is by this that the greatest part of the human race has been civilized; an advantage which the New Zealanders, from their situation, never had. An intercourse with foreigners would reform their manners and polish their savage minds. Or were they united under a settled form of government, they would have fewer enemies; consequently this custom would be less in use, and might in time be in a manner forgotten. At present they have but little idea of treating others as they themselves would *wish* to be treated, but treat them as they *expect* to be treated. If I remember right, one of the arguments they made use of to Tupia [a native of Tahiti], who frequently expostulated with them against this custom, was that there could be no harm in killing and eating the man who would do the same by them if it was in his power. "For," said they, "can there be any harm in eating our enemies, whom we have killed in battle? Would not those very enemies have done the same to us?" I have often seen them listen to Tupia with great attention, but I never found his arguments have any weight with them, or that, with all his rhetoric, he could persuade any one of them that this custom was wrong.

### 5. THE SOUTHERN ICE IN 1774

January 26th, 1774. We had nine small ice islands in sight; and soon after we came the third time within the antarctic polar circle, in the longitude of 109° 31′ west. About noon, seeing the appearance of land to the s.e., we immediately trimmed our sails and stood towards it. Soon after it disappeared, but we did not give it up till eight o'clock the next morning, when we were well assured that it was nothing but clouds or a fog bank; and then we resumed our course to the south, with a gentle breeze at n.e., attended with a thick fog, snow, and sleet.

January 28th. We had so thick a fog that we could not see two hundred yards round us; and as we knew not the extent of the loose ice, I durst not steer to the south till we had clear weather. Thus we spent the night, or rather that part of the twenty-four hours which answered to night; for we had no darkness but what was occasioned by fogs.

January 30th. At four o'clock in the morning we perceived the clouds over the horizon to the south to be of an unusual snow-white brightness, which we knew announced our approach to field-ice. Soon after it was seen from the top-mast head; and at eight o'clock we were close to its edge. It extended east and west far beyond the reach of our sight. In the situation we were in, just the southern half of our horizon was illuminated by the rays of light reflected from the ice, to a considerable height. Ninety-seven ice hills were distinctly seen within the field, besides those on the outside, many of them very large, and looking like a ridge of mountains rising one above another till they were lost in the clouds. The outer or northern edge of this immense field was composed of loose or broken ice close packed together, so that it was not possible for anything to enter it. This was about a mile broad; and within it was solid ice in one continued compact body. It was rather low and flat, except the hills, but seemed to increase in height as we traced it to the south, in which direction it extended beyond our sight. Such mountains of ice as these were, I believe, never seen in the Greenland seas— at least, not that I ever heard or read of; so that we cannot draw a comparison between the ice here and that there. It must be allowed that these pro- digious ice mountains must add such weight to the ice fields that enclose them, as cannot but make a great difference between navigating this icy sea and navigating that of Greenland.

We were now in the latitude of 71° 10′ south. I will not say it was impossible anywhere to get farther to the south; but the attempting it would have been a dangerous and rash enterprise, and what, I believe, no man in my situation would have thought of. It was indeed my opinion, as well as the opinion of most on board, that this ice extended quite to the pole, or perhaps joined to some land to which it had been fixed from the earliest time; and that it is here, that is to the south of this parallel, where all the ice is first formed that we find scattered up and down to the north, and afterwards broken off, by gales of wind or other causes, and brought to the north by the currents, which we always found to set in that direction in the high latitudes.

As we drew near this ice some penguins were heard, but none seen, and but few other birds or any other thing that could induce us to think any land was near. And yet I think there must be some land to the south behind this ice; but if there is, it can afford no better retreat for birds or any other animals than the ice itself, with which it must be wholly covered. I, who had ambition not only to go farther than anyone had been before, but as far as it was possible for man to go, was not sorry at meeting with this interruption, as it in some measure relieved us; at least it shortened the dangers and hardships inseparable from the navigation of the southern polar regions. Since, therefore, we could not proceed one inch farther to the south, no other reason need be assigned for my tacking and standing back to the north.

It was happy for us that the weather was clear when we fell in with this ice, and that we discovered it so soon as we did; for we had no sooner tacked than we were involved in a thick fog. At noon the mercury in the thermometer stood at $32\frac{1}{2}°$, and we found the air exceedingly cold. The thick fog continuing, with showers of snow, gave a coat of ice to our rigging of near an inch thick. In the afternoon of the next day the fog cleared away at intervals, but the weather was cloudy and gloomy, and the air excessively cold; however, the sea within our horizon was clear of ice.

### 6. EASTER ISLAND

March 14th, 1774. I went ashore, accompanied by some of the gentlemen, to see what the island was likely to afford us. We landed at a sandy beach, where some hundreds of the natives were assembled, who were so impatient to see us that many of them swam off to meet the boats. Not one of them had so much as a stick or weapon of any sort in his hands. After distributing a few trinkets among them, we made signs for something to eat, on which they brought down a few potatoes, plantains, and sugar-canes, and exchanged them for nails, looking-glasses, and pieces of cloth.

We presently discovered that they were as expert thieves and as tricking in their exchanges as any people we had yet met with. It was with some difficulty that we could keep the hats on our heads, but it was hardly possible to keep anything in our pockets, not even what themselves had sold us; for they would watch every opportunity to snatch it from us, so that we sometimes bought the same thing two or three times over, and after all did not get it.

March 15th. I sent two lieutenants with a party of men, accompanied by several of the gentlemen, to examine the country. As I was not sufficiently recovered from my late illness to make one of the party, I was obliged to content myself with remaining at the landing-place among the natives. We had at one time a pretty brisk trade with them for potatoes, which we observed they dug up out of an adjoining plantation; but this traffic, which was very advantageous to us, was soon put a stop to by the owner (as we supposed) of the plantation coming down and driving all the people out of it. By this we concluded that he had been robbed of his property, and that they were not more scrupulous of stealing from one another than from us, on whom they practised every little fraud they could think of, and generally with success.

About seven o'clock in the evening the party I had sent into the country returned, after having been over the greatest part of the island. They left the beach about nine o'clock in the morning, and took a path which led across to the s.e. side of the island, followed by a great crowd of the natives, who pressed much upon them. But they had not proceeded far before a middle-aged man, punctured from head to foot, and with his face painted with a sort of white pigment, appeared with a spear in his hand, and walked alongside of them, making signs to his countrymen to keep at a distance and not to molest our people. When he had pretty well effected this, he hoisted a piece of white cloth on his spear, placed himself in the front, and led the way with his ensign of peace, as they understood it to be.

On the east side, near the sea, they met with three platforms of stone-work, or rather the ruins of them. On each had stood four large statues, but they were all fallen down from two of them, and also one from the third; all except one were broken by the fall, or in some measure defaced. The unbroken one was measured, and found to be fifteen feet in length and six feet broad over the shoulders.

Each statue had on its head a large cylindric stone of a red colour, wrought perfectly round. The one measured, which was not by far the largest, was fifty-two inches high and fifty-six in diameter. In some the upper corner of the cylinder was taken off in a sort of concave quarter-round, but in others the cylinder was entire.

They passed some huts, the owners of which met them with roasted potatoes and sugar-canes, and placing themselves ahead of the foremost of the party—for they marched in line in order to have the benefit of the path—gave one to each man as he passed by. They observed the same method in distributing the water which they brought, and were particularly careful that the foremost did not drink too much, lest none should be left for the hindmost. But at the very time these were relieving the thirsty and hungry, there were not wanting others who endeavoured to steal from them the very things which had been given them. At last, to prevent worse consequences, they were obliged to fire a load of small shot at one who was so audacious as to snatch from one of the men the bag which contained everything they carried with them. The shot hit him on the back; but he afterwards got up and walked, and what became of him they knew not, nor whether he was much wounded.

As this affair caused some delay, and drew the natives together, they presently saw the man who had hitherto led the way, and one or two more, coming running towards them; but instead of stopping when they came up, they continued to run round them, repeating, in a kind manner, a few words, until our people set forwards again. Then their old guide hoisted his flag, leading the way as before, and none ever attempted to steal from them the whole day afterwards.

Towards the eastern end of the island they met with a well whose water was perfectly fresh, being considerably above the level of the sea; but it was dirty, owing to the filthiness or cleanliness (call it which you will) of the natives, who never go to drink without washing themselves all over as soon as they have done; and if ever so many of them are together, the first leaps right into the middle of the hole, drinks, and washes himself without the least ceremony, after which another takes his place and does the same.

They observed that this side of the island was full of those gigantic statues before-mentioned, some placed in groups on platforms of masonry, others single, fixed only in the earth, and that not deeply; and these latter are, in general, much larger than the others. Having measured one which had fallen down, they found it very near twenty-seven feet long and upwards of eight feet over the breast or shoulders; and yet this appeared considerably short of the size of one they saw standing, its shade, a little past two o'clock, being sufficient to shelter all the party, consisting of near thirty persons, from the rays of the sun.

In a small hollow on the highest part of the island they met with several such cylinders as are placed on the heads of the statues. Some of these appeared larger than any they had seen before; but it was then too late to stop to measure them. The gentleman from whom I had this information is of opinion that there had been a quarry here, whence these stones had formerly been dug, and that it would have been no difficult matter to roll them down the hill after they were formed. I think this a very reasonable conjecture, and have no doubt that it has been so.

The gigantic statues are not, in my opinion, looked upon as idols by the present inhabitants; at least, I saw nothing that could induce me to think so. On the contrary, I rather suppose that they are burying-places for certain tribes or families. I, as well as some others, saw a human skeleton lying in one of the platforms, just covered with stones.

Some of these platforms of masonry are thirty or

forty feet long, twelve or sixteen broad, and from three to twelve in height, this last in some measure depending on the nature of the ground. For they are generally at the brink of the bank facing the sea, so that this face may be ten or twelve feet or more high, and the other may be not above three or four. They are built, or rather faced, with hewn stones of a very large size; and the workmanship is not inferior to the best plain piece of masonry we have in England. They use no sort of cement; yet the joints are exceedingly close, and the stones morticed and tenanted one into another in a very artful manner. The side walls are not vertical, but incline a little inwards, in the same manner that breast-works, &c., are built in Europe; yet had not all this care, pains, and sagacity been able to preserve these curious structures from the ravages of all-devouring Time.

The statues, or at least many of them, are erected on these platforms, which serve as foundations. They are, as near as we could judge, about half-length, ending in a sort of stump at the bottom, on which they stand. The workmanship is rude, but not bad; nor are the features of the face ill-formed, the nose and chin in particular; but the ears are long beyond proportion; and as to the bodies, there is hardly anything like a human figure about them.

M 738

EXAMINING THE STATUES ON EASTER ISLAND

I had an opportunity of examining only two or three of these statues which are near the landing-place; and they were of a gray stone, seemingly of the same sort as that with which the platforms were built. But some of the gentlemen, who travelled over the island and examined many of them, were of opinion that the stone of which they were made was different from any other they saw on the island, and had much the appearance of being artificial. We could hardly conceive how these islanders, wholly unacquainted with any mechanical power, could raise such stupendous figures, and afterwards place the large cylindric stones before-mentioned upon their heads. The only method I can conceive is by raising the upper end by little and little, supporting it by stones as it is raised, and building about it till they got it erect; thus a sort of mount or scaffolding would be made, upon which they might roll the cylinder, and place it upon the head of the statue, and then the stones might be removed from about it. But if the stones are artificial, the statues might have been put to-gether on the place, in their present position, and the cylinder put on by building a mount round them as above-mentioned. But let them have been made and set up by this or any other method, they must have been a work of immense time, and sufficiently show the ingenuity and perseverance of the islanders in the age in which they were built; for the present inhabitants have most certainly had no hand in them, as they do not even repair the foundations of those which are going to decay.

Besides these monuments of antiquity, which were pretty numerous, and nowhere but on or near the sea-coast, there were many little heaps of stones piled up in different places along the coast. Two or three of the uppermost stones in each pile were generally white, perhaps always so when the pile is complete. It will hardly be doubted that these piles of stones had a meaning. Probably they might mark the place where people had been buried, and serve instead of the large statues.

### 7. AN INCIDENT AT THE NEW HEBRIDES

July 22nd, 1774. In the morning a good many natives came round us, some in canoes and some swimming. I soon prevailed on one to come on board; which he no sooner did than he was followed by more than I desired; so that not only our deck, but the rigging, was presently filled with them. I took four into the cabin and gave them various articles, which they showed to those in the canoes, and seemed much pleased with their reception. While I was thus making friends with those in the cabin, an accident happened that threw all into confusion, but in the end, I believe, proved advantageous to us.

A fellow in a canoe, having been refused admission into one of our boats that lay alongside, bent his bow to shoot a poisoned arrow at the boat-keeper. Some of his countrymen prevented his doing it at that instant, and gave time to acquaint me with it. I ran instantly on deck, and saw another man struggling with him, one of those who had been in the cabin, and had leapt out of the window for this purpose. The other seemed resolved, shook him off, and directed his bow again to the boat-keeper, but on my calling to him pointed it at me. Having a musket in my hand loaded with small shot, I gave him the contents. This staggered him for a moment, but did not prevent him from holding his bow still in the attitude of shooting. Another discharge of the same nature made him drop it, and the others who were in the canoe to paddle off with all speed. At this time some began to shoot arrows on the other side. A musket discharged in the air had no effect, but a four-pounder shot over their heads sent them off in the utmost confusion. Many quitted their canoes and swam on shore; those in the great cabin leaped out of the windows;

and those who were on the deck and on various parts of the rigging all leaped overboard. After this we took no further notice of them, but suffered them to come off and pick up their canoes; and some even ventured again alongside the ship. Immediately after the great gun was fired we heard the beating of drums on shore, which was, probably, the signal for the country to assemble in arms. We now got everything in readiness to land, to cut some wood, which we were in want of, and to try to get some refreshments, nothing of this kind having been seen in any of the canoes.

About nine o'clock we put off in two boats, and landed in the face of four or five hundred people, who were assembled on the shore. Though they were all armed with bows and arrows, clubs, and spears, they made not the least opposition. On the contrary, seeing me advance alone, with nothing but a green branch in my hand, one of them, who seemed to be a chief, giving his bow and arrows to another, met me in the water, bearing also a green branch, which having exchanged for the one I held, he then took me by the hand and led me up to the crowd. I immediately distributed presents to them, and, in the meantime, the marines were drawn up upon the beach. I then made signs—for we understood not a word of their language—that we wanted wood; and they made signs to us to cut down the trees. By this time a small pig was brought down and presented to me; I gave the bearer a piece of cloth, with which he seemed well pleased. This made us hope that we should have some more, but we were mistaken. The pig was not brought to be exchanged for what we had, but on some other account, probably as a peace-offering. For all we could do or say did not prevail on them to bring down, after this, above half a dozen cocoa-nuts, and a small quantity of fresh water. They set no value on nails or any sort of iron tools, nor indeed on anything we had. They would now and then exchange an arrow for a piece of cloth, but very seldom would part with a bow. They were very unwilling we should go off the beach, and very desirous we should return on board. At length, about noon, after sending on board what wood we had cut, we embarked ourselves; and they all retired, some one way and some another.

Had we made a longer stay, we might soon have been upon good terms with this ape-like nation. For, in general, they are the most ugly, ill-proportioned people I ever saw, and in every respect different from any we had met with in this sea. They are a very dark-coloured and rather diminutive race, with long heads, flat faces, and monkey countenances. Their hair, mostly black or brown, is short and curly, but not quite so soft and woolly as that of a negro. Their beards are very strong, crisp, and bushy, and generally black and short. But what most adds to their deformity is a belt or cord which they wear round the waist, and tie so tight over the belly that the shape of their bodies is not unlike that of an overgrown ant. The men go quite naked, except for a piece of cloth or a leaf used as an apron. We saw but few women, and they were not less ugly than the men. Their heads, faces, and shoulders are painted red. They wear a kind of petticoat, and some of them had something over their shoulders like a bag, in which they carry their children. Their ornaments are ear-rings made of tortoise-shell, and bracelets. A curious one of the latter, four or five inches broad, wrought with thread or cord, and studded with shells, is worn by them just above the elbow. Round the right wrist they wear hogs' tusks, bent circular, and rings made of shells; and round the left, a round piece of wood, which we judged was to ward off the bow-string. The bridge of the nose is pierced, and in it they wear a piece of white stone, about an inch and a half long, and bent into a curve. As signs of friendship they present a green branch, and sprinkle water with the hand over the head.

Their weapons are clubs, spears, and bows and arrows. The two former are made of hard or iron-wood. Their bows are about four feet long, made of a stick split down the middle, and are of irregular curvature. The arrows, which are a sort of reeds, are sometimes armed with a long and sharp point, made of the hard wood, and sometimes with a very hard point made of bone; and these points are all covered with a substance which we took for poison. Indeed, the people themselves confirmed our suspicions, by making signs to us not to touch the point, and giving us to understand that if we were pricked by them we should die. They are very careful of them themselves, and keep them always wrapped up in a quiver. Some of these arrows are armed with two or three points, each with small prickles on the edge to prevent the arrow being drawn out of the wound.

### 8. NEW CALEDONIA

September 4th, 1774. At eight o'clock, as we were steering to the south, land was discovered. We continued to steer for it with a light breeze at east, till five in the evening, when we were stopped by a calm. At this time we were three leagues from the land. Some openings appeared in the west, so that we could not tell whether it was one connected land or a group of islands. Breakers were seen about half-way between us and the shore, and behind them two or three canoes under sail, standing out to sea, as if their design had been to come off to us; but a little before sunset they struck their sails, and we saw them no more.

On the 5th some gaps or openings were yet to be seen to the west, and a reef, or breakers, seemed to lie all along the coast, connected with those we discovered the preceding night. We bore down to the N.W., and after running two leagues down the outside of the reef, we came before an opening that had the appearance of a good channel through which we might go in for the land. I wanted to get at it, not only to visit it, but also to have an opportunity to observe an eclipse of the sun which was soon to happen. We now saw that what we had taken for openings in the coast was low land, and that it was all connected except the western extremity, which was a separate island.

After dinner I went on shore with two armed boats, having with us one of the natives who had attached himself to me. We landed on a sandy beach before a vast number of people, who had got together with no other intent than to see us, for many of them had not a stick in their hands.

Consequently we were received with great courtesy, and with the surprise natural for people to express at seeing men and things so new to them as we must have been. I made presents to all those my friend pointed out, who were either old men, or such as seemed to be of some note; but he took not the least notice of some women who stood behind the crowd, holding my hands when I was going to give them some beads and medals. Here we found a chief who had been seen in one of the canoes in the morning; and we had not been on shore above ten minutes when he called for silence. Being instantly obeyed by every individual present, he made a short speech; and soon after another chief, having called for silence, made a speech also. It was pleasing to see with what attention they were heard. Their speeches were composed of short sentences, to each of which two or three old men answered, by nodding their heads, and giving a kind of grunt, significant, as I thought, of appro-bation. It was impossible for us to know the purport of these speeches, but we had reason to think they were favourable to us, on whose account they doubtless were made. I kept my eyes fixed on the people all the time, and saw nothing to induce me to think otherwise.

On the 7th a party of us went to take a view of

the country. As soon as we landed, we made known our design to the natives, and two of them, undertaking to be our guides, conducted us up the hills by a tolerably good path. In our route we met several people, most of whom turned back with us, so that at last our train was numerous. Some we met who wanted us to return; but we paid no regard to their signs, nor did they seem uneasy when we proceeded. At length we reached the summit of one of the hills, from which we saw the sea in two places, between some advanced hills on the opposite or s.w. side of the island. This was a useful discovery, as it enabled us to judge of the breadth of the land, which in this part did not exceed ten leagues.

Between those advanced hills and the ridge we were upon was a large valley, through which ran a serpentine river. On the banks of this were several plantations and some villages, whose inhabitants we had met on the road. The plain or flat land, which lies along the shore we were upon, appeared from the hills to great advantage; the winding streams that ran through it, the plantations, the little straggling villages, the variety in the woods, and the shoals on the coast, so variegating the scene that the whole might afford a picture for romance. Indeed, if it were not for those fertile spots and some few on the sides of the mountains, the whole country might be called a dreary waste. The mountains and other high parts are, for the most part, incapable of cultivation. The little soil that is upon them is scorched and burnt up with the sun; it is, nevertheless, coated with coarse grass and other plants, and here and there trees and shrubs. The country, in general, bore great resemblance to some parts of New Holland [Australia] under the same parallel of latitude, several of its natural productions seeming to be the same, and the woods being without underwood, as in that country. The reefs on the coast and several other similarities were obvious to every one who had seen both countries. We observed all the N.E. coast to be covered with shoals and breakers, extending to the northward till they were lost in the horizon.

In the afternoon of the 12th I went on shore, and, on a large tree which stood close to the shore near the watering-place, had an inscription cut, setting forth the ship's name, date, &c., as a testimony of our being the first discoverers of this country, as I had done at all others at which we had touched where this ceremony was necessary.

On this island the houses, or at least most of them, are circular, something like a bee-hive, and full as close and warm. The entrance is by a small door or long square hole, just big enough to admit a man bent double. The side-walls are about four feet and a half high; but the roof is lofty, and peaked to a point at the top, above which is a post or stick of wood, which is generally ornamented with carving or shells, or both. The framing is of small spars, reeds, &c., and both sides and roof are thick and close covered with thatch, made of long coarse grass. In the inside of the house are set up posts, to which cross spars are fastened, and so platforms made, for the conveniency of laying anything on. Some houses have two floors, one above the other. The floor is laid with dry grass, and here and there mats are spread, for the principal people to sleep or sit on. In most of them we found two fireplaces, and commonly a fire burning; and, as there was no vent for the smoke but by the door, the whole house was both smoky and hot, insomuch that we, who were not used to such an atmosphere, could hardly endure it a moment. This may be the reason why we found these people so chilly when in the open air and without exercise. We frequently saw them make little fires anywhere, and hustle round them, with no other view than to warm themselves. Smoke within doors may be a necessary evil, as it prevents the mosquitoes from coming in, which are pretty numerous here.

In some respects their habitations are neat; for besides the ornaments at top, I saw some with carved door-posts. Upon the whole, their houses are better calculated for a cold than for a hot climate; and as there are no partitions in them, they can have little privacy.

They have no great variety of household utensils, earthen jars being the only article worth notice. Each family has at least one of them, in which they bake their roots and perhaps their fish. The fire by which they cook their victuals is on the outside of each house in the open air. There are three or four pointed stones fixed in the ground, their pointed ends being about six inches above the ground. Sets of three stones are only for one jar, those of five stones for two jars. The jars do not stand on their bottoms, but lie inclined on their sides. The use of the stones is, obviously, to keep the jars from resting on the fire, in order that it may burn the better.

They subsist chiefly on roots and fish, and the bark of a tree which I am told grows also in the West Indies. This they roast, and are almost continually chewing. It has a sweetish, insipid taste, and was liked by some of our people. Water is their only liquor; at least I never saw any other made use of. Plantains and sugar-canes are by no means in plenty. Bread-fruit is scarce, and the cocoa-nut trees are small and but thinly planted, and neither one nor the other seems to yield much fruit.

## 9. CHRISTMAS SOUND, IN TIERRA DEL FUEGO

December 24th, 1774. We made up two shooting parties. As soon as we got under the island we found plenty of shags in the cliffs, but without staying to spend our time and shot upon these, we proceeded on, and presently found sport enough. For in the south side of the island was abundance of geese. It happened to be the moulting season, and most of them were on shore for that reason, and could not fly. There being a great surf, we found great difficulty in landing, and very bad climbing over the rocks when we were landed, so that hundreds of the geese escaped us, some into the sea, and others up into the island. We, however, by one means or another got sixty-two, with which we returned on board, heartily tired; but the acquisition we had made overbalanced every other consideration, and we sat down with a good appetite to supper on what the preceding day had produced. The other party had got on board some time before us with sixteen geese, so that I was able to make distribution to the whole crew, which

was the more acceptable on account of the approaching festival. For, had not Providence thus
singularly provided for us, our Christmas cheer
must have been salt beef and pork.

I now learned that a number of the natives in
nine canoes had been alongside the ship, and some
on board. The next morning, the 25th, they made
us another visit. They are a little, ugly, half-
starved, beardless race. I saw not a tall person
amongst them. They were almost naked. Their
clothing was of seal-skin; some had two or three
sewed together so as to make a cloak which reached
to the knees; but the most of them had only one
skin, hardly large enough to cover their shoulders.
They had with them bows and arrows, and darts,
or rather harpoons, made of bone and fitted to a
staff. I suppose they were intended to kill seals
and fish; they may also kill whales with them as
the Esquimaux do. I know not if they resemble
them in their love of train-oil, but they and everything they had smelt most intolerably of it. I
ordered them some biscuit, but did not observe
them very fond of it. They were much better
pleased when I gave them some medals and knives.

The women and children remained in the canoes.
These were made of bark; and in each was a fire,
over which the poor creatures huddled themselves.

I cannot suppose that they carry a fire in their canoes for this purpose only, but rather that it may be always ready to remove ashore whenever they land; for let their method of obtaining fire be what it may, they cannot be always sure of obtaining dry fuel that will kindle from a spark. They likewise carry in their canoes large seal hides, which I judged were to shelter them when at sea, to serve as covering for their huts on shore, and occasionally to be used as sails.

They all retired before dinner, and did not wait to partake of our Christmas cheer. Indeed, I believe no one invited them, and for good reasons; for their dirty persons, and the stench they carried about them, were enough to spoil the appetite of any European, and that would have been a real disappointment, as we had not experienced such fare for some time. Roast and boiled geese, goose-pie, &c., was a treat little known to us; and we had yet some Madeira wine left, which was the only article of our provision that mended by keeping. So that our friends in England did not, perhaps, celebrate Christmas more cheerfully than we did. The festival which we celebrated at this place occasioned my giving it the name of Christmas Sound.

## 10. IN THE FAR SOUTH ATLANTIC, 1775

[Leaving Staten Land at the beginning of January, 1775, Cook steered to the east and then to the south. Several pieces of land had been reported thereabouts, and he wished to learn whether they were parts of a "Southern Continent".]

January 12th.   At noon observed in lat. 54° 28′ south, long. 42° 8′ west; we had no other signs of land than seeing a seal and a few penguins; on the contrary we had a swell from E.S.E., which would hardly have been if any extensive tract of land lay in that direction.

Jan. 13th.   The calm, attended by a thick fog, continued till six next morning.   We stood to the south till noon; saw several penguins and a snow petrel, which we looked on to be signs of the vicinity of ice.   The air, too, was much colder than we had felt it since we left New Zealand.

Jan. 14th.   At nine in the morning we saw an island of ice, as we then thought, but at noon we were doubtful whether it was ice or land.   At two p.m. it was no longer doubted that it was land and not ice that we had in sight.   It was, however, in a manner wholly covered with snow.   We were further confirmed in our judgment of its being land by finding soundings at one hundred and seventy-five fathoms, with a muddy bottom.   [The land was the N.W. point of South Georgia.]

Jan. 15th. The wind blew in squalls, attended with snow and sleet, and we had a great sea to encounter.

Jan. 16th. At this time we had a great swell from the south, an indication that no land was near us in that direction; nevertheless the vast quantity of snow on that in sight induced us to think it was extensive, and I chose to begin with exploring the northern coast.

Jan. 17th. At two o'clock in the morning we made sail in for the land. We steered along shore, at the distance of four or five miles, till seven o'clock, when, seeing the appearance of an inlet, we hauled in for it. As soon as we drew near the shore, having hoisted out a boat, I embarked in it, accompanied by Mr. Forster, the naturalist, and his party, with a view to reconnoitring the bay before we ventured in with the ship. But when I came to a resolution not to bring the ship in, I did not examine the places where I judged there might be good anchorage, for it did not seem probable that anyone would ever be benefited by the discovery. I landed in three different places, displayed our colours, and took possession of the country in His Majesty's name, under a discharge of small-arms.

The head of the bay, as well as two places on

each side, was terminated by vertical ice-cliffs of considerable height. Pieces were continually breaking off, and floating out to sea; and a great fall happened while we were in the bay, and made a noise like cannon.

The inner parts of the country were not less savage and horrible. The wild rocks raised their lofty summits till they were lost in the clouds, and the valleys lay covered with everlasting snow. Not a tree was to be seen, nor a shrub even big enough to make a toothpick. The only vegetation we met with was a coarse strong-bladed grass growing in tufts, wild burnet, and a plant like moss, which sprang from the rocks.

Seals, or sea-bears, were pretty numerous. Perhaps the most of those we saw were females; for the shores swarmed with young cubs. Here were several flocks of penguins, the largest I ever saw; some that we brought on board weighed from twenty-nine to thirty-eight pounds. There were also many oceanic birds, such as albatrosses, and gulls of various kinds. All the land birds we saw consisted of a few small larks; nor did we meet with any quadrupeds, though Mr. Forster saw traces of what he judged to be a fox, or some such animal.

Having made these observations, we set out for the ship, and got on board a little after twelve o'clock, with a quantity of seals and penguins, an acceptable present to the crew. It must not, however, be understood that we were in want of provisions, for we had plenty of every kind; but any kind of fresh meat was preferred by most on board to salt. For my own part, I was now, for the first time, heartily tired of salt meat of every kind; and though the flesh of the penguins could scarcely vie with bullock's liver, its being fresh was sufficient to make it go down. I called the bay we had been in Possession Bay.

[They coasted the island to its southern extremity.]

On the 20th our observations proved that this land, which we had taken for part of a great continent, was no more than an island of seventy leagues in circuit.

Who would have thought that an island of no greater extent than this, situated between the latitudes of 54° and 55°, should, in the very height of summer, be, in a manner, wholly covered many fathoms deep with frozen snow? The very sides and craggy summits of the lofty mountains were cased in snow and ice; but the quantity that lay in the valleys is incredible; and at the bottom of the bays the coast was terminated by a wall of ice of considerable height. It can hardly be doubted that a great deal of ice is formed here in the winter, which in the spring is broken off and dispersed over the sea; but this island cannot produce the ten-thousandth part of what we saw; so that either there must be more land, or the ice is formed without it. These reflections led me to think that the land we had just seen might belong to an extensive tract; and I still had hopes of discovering a continent. I must confess the disappointment I now met with did not affect me much; for, to judge of the bulk by the sample, it would not be worth the discovery.

I called this land the Isle of Georgia in honour of His Majesty King George III. It seems to abound with bays and harbours, the N.E. coast especially; but the vast quantity of ice must render them inaccessible the greater part of the year; or, at least, it must be dangerous lying in them on account of the breaking up of the ice-cliffs. It is remarkable that we did not see a river or stream of fresh water on the whole coast. I think it highly probable that there are no perennial springs in the country, and that the interior parts, being much elevated, never enjoy heat enough to melt the snow in such quantities as to produce a river or stream of water.

We continued to steer to the south till the 27th. I now reckoned we were in latitude 60° south, and

farther I did not intend to go, unless I observed
some certain signs of soon meeting with land. I was
tired of these high southern latitudes, where nothing
was to be found but ice and thick fogs. We had
now a long hollow swell from the west, a strong
indication that there was no land in that direction.

January 28th. We continued to stand to the
east till half-past two o'clock p.m., when we fell in,
all at once, with a vast number of large ice islands,
and a sea strewed with loose ice. The weather,
too, was become thick and hazy, attended with
drizzling rain and sleet, which made it the more
dangerous to stand in among the ice. The ice
islands which at this time surrounded us were
nearly all of equal height, and showed a flat, even
surface; but they were of various extent, some
being two or three miles in circuit. The loose ice
was what had broken from these isles.

January 31st. The fog very fortunately clearing away a little, we discovered land ahead, three
or four miles distant. It proved to be three rocky
islets of considerable height, and behind them
appeared an elevated coast, whose lofty snow-clad
summits were seen above the clouds. I called
this land Southern Thule, because it is the most
southern land that has ever yet been discovered.
Finding that we could not weather Thule, we

tacked and stood to the north, and at four our first islet bore east, distant three or four leagues.

[February 1st, 2nd, and 3rd, they several times saw similar appearances of land.]

February 6th. Seeing neither land nor signs of any, I concluded that what we had seen, which I named Sandwich Land, was either a group of islands, or else a point of the continent. For I firmly believe that there is a tract of land near the pole which is the source of most of the ice that is spread over this vast Southern Ocean. I also think it probable that it extends farthest to the north opposite the Southern Atlantic and Indian Oceans, because ice was always found by us farther to the north in these oceans than anywhere else, which I judge could not be if there were not land to the south; I mean a land of considerable extent. Very few ships have met with ice in going round Cape Horn; and we saw but little below the sixtieth degree of latitude in the Southern Pacific Ocean. Whereas in this ocean, between the meridian of 40° west and 50° or 60° east, we found ice as far north as 51°, and others have seen it in a much lower latitude.

It is true, however, that the greatest part of this southern continent (supposing there is one) must lie within the polar circle, where the sea is so pestered with ice that the land is thereby inaccessible. The risk one runs in exploring a coast in these unknown and icy seas is so very great, that I can be bold enough to say that no man will ever venture farther than I have done; and that the lands which may lie to the south will never be explored. Thick fogs, snow-storms, intense cold, and every other thing that can render navigation dangerous must be encountered; and these difficulties are greatly heightened by the inexpressibly horrid aspect of the country, a country doomed by nature never once to feel the warmth of the sun's rays, but to lie buried in everlasting snow and ice. The ports which may be on the coast are, in a manner, wholly filled up with snow of vast thickness; but if any should be so far open as to invite a ship into it, she would run a risk of being fixed there for ever, or of coming out in an ice island.

After such an explanation as this, the reader must not expect to find me much farther to the south. It would have been rashness in me to have risked all that had been done during the voyage, in discovering and exploring a coast, which, when discovered and explored, would have answered no end whatever, or have been of the least use, either to navigation or to geography, or indeed to any other science.

These reasons induced me to alter the course to east, with a very strong gale at north, attended with an exceedingly heavy fall of snow. The quantity that lodged in our sails was so great that we were frequently obliged to throw the ship up in the wind, to shake it out of them; otherwise neither they nor the ship could have supported the weight.

## 11. THE ISLANDS OF ST. HELENA AND ASCENSION

At daybreak in the morning of the 15th of May, 1775, we saw the island of St. Helena at the distance of fourteen leagues; and at midnight anchored in the road before the town, on the N.W. side of the island. At sunrise the next morning the castle saluted us with thirteen guns; on my landing, soon after, I was saluted by the castle with the same number; and each of the salutes was returned by the ship.

The Governor and the principal gentlemen of the island received and treated me, during my stay, with the greatest politeness, by showing me every kind of civility in their power.

Whoever views St. Helena in its present state, and can but conceive what it must have been originally, will not hastily charge the inhabitants with want of industry, though perhaps they might

apply it to more advantage were more land appropriated to planting of corn, vegetables, roots, &c.,
instead of being laid out in pasture, which is the
present mode.  But this is not likely to happen so
long as the greatest part of it remains in the hands
of the East India Company and their servants.
Without industrious planters this island can never
flourish and be in a condition to supply the ship-
ping with the necessary refreshments.

During our stay here we finished some necessary
repairs of the ship which we had not time to do at
the Cape.  We also filled all our empty water-
casks; and the crew were served with fresh beef,
purchased at fivepence per pound.  Their beef is
exceedingly good, and is the only refreshment to
be had worth mentioning.

On the 21st, in the evening, I took leave of the
Governor, and repaired on board.  Upon my leaving the shore I was saluted with thirteen guns,
and upon my getting under sail I was saluted with
thirteen more, both of which I returned.

In the morning of the 28th I made the island of
Ascension, and the same evening anchored in Cross
Bay on the N.W. side, in ten fathoms water.  We
remained here till the evening of the 31st, and
notwithstanding we had several parties out every
night, we got but twenty-four turtle, it being

rather too late in the season.  However, as they weighed between four and five hundred pounds each, we thought ourselves not ill off.  We might have had a plentiful supply of fish in general, but the catching of any of these was not attended to, the object being turtle.

The island of Ascension is about ten miles in length and about five or six in breadth.  It shows a surface composed of barren hills and valleys, on the most of which not a shrub or plant is to be seen for several miles, and where we found nothing but stones and sand, or rather slag and ashes, an indubitable sign that the isle, at some remote time, has been destroyed [rather, *formed*] by a volcano, which has thrown up vast heaps of stones, and even hills.  Between these heaps of stones we found a smooth, even surface, composed of ashes and sand, and very good travelling upon it.  But one may as easily walk over broken glass bottles as over the stones; if the foot deceives you, you are sure to be cut or lamed, and this happened to some of our people.

There is a high mountain at the S.E. end of the isle, whose soil is a kind of white marl possessing vegetative qualities, and producing a kind of purslane, spurge, and one or two grasses.  On these the goats subsist, and it is at this part of the isle where they are to be found, as also land-crabs, which are said to be very good.

I was told that about this part of the isle is some very good land, on which might be raised many necessary articles; and some have been at the trouble of sowing turnips and other useful vegetables. I was also told that there is a fine spring in a valley which separates two hills on the top of the mountain above-mentioned, besides great quantities of fresh water in holes in the rocks, which the person who gave me this information believed was collected from rains.

Turtle, I am told, can be found at this isle from January to June. The method of catching them is to have people upon the several sandy bays to watch their coming on shore to lay their eggs, which is always in the night, and then turn them on their backs, till there be an opportunity to take them off the next day. It was recommended to us to send a good many men to each beach, where they were to lie quiet till the turtle were ashore, and then rise and turn them at once. This method may be the best when the turtle are numerous; but when there are but few, three or four men are sufficient for the largest beach; and if they keep patrolling it close to the wash of the surf during the night, by this method they will see all that come ashore, and cause less noise than if there were more of them. It was by this method we caught the most we got; and this is the method by which the Americans take them. Nothing is more certain than that all the turtle which are found about this island come here for the sole purpose of laying their eggs; for we met with none but females; and of all those that we caught not one had any food worth mentioning in its stomach; a sure sign, in my opinion, that they must have been a long time without any; and this may be the reason why the flesh of them is not so good as that of some I have eaten on the coast of New South Wales, which were caught on the spot where they fed.

### 12. COOK'S CARE FOR THE HEALTH OF HIS MEN

Having been absent from England three years and eighteen days, in which time and under all changes of climate I lost but four men, and only one of them by sickness, it may not be amiss to enumerate the several causes to which, under the care of Providence, I conceive this uncommon good state of health was owing.

We were furnished with a quantity of malt, of which was made *Sweet Wort*. To such of the men as showed the least symptoms of the scurvy, and also to such as were thought to be threatened with that disorder, this was given, from one to three pints a day for each man, or in such proportion as the surgeon found necessary, which sometimes amounted to three quarts. This is, without doubt, one of the best antiscorbutic sea-medicines yet discovered; and if used in time will, with proper attention to other things, I am persuaded, prevent the scurvy from making any great progress for a considerable while. But I am not altogether of opinion that it will cure it at sea.

*Sour Krout*, of which we had a large quantity, is not only a wholesome vegetable food, but, in my judgment, highly antiscorbutic; and it spoils not by keeping. A pound of this was served to each, when at sea, twice a week, or oftener, as was thought necessary.

*Portable Broth* was another great article, of which we had a large supply. An ounce of this to each man, or such other proportion as circumstances pointed out, was boiled in their pease, three days in the week; and when we were in places where vegetables were to be got, it was boiled with them, and wheat or oatmeal every morning for breakfast; and also with pease and vegetables for dinner. It enabled us to make several nourishing and whole-some messes, and was the means of making the people eat a greater quantity of vegetables than they would otherwise have done.

*Rob* [concentrated juice] *of Lemon and Orange* is an antiscorbutic we were not without. The surgeon made use of it in many cases with great success.

Amongst the articles of victualling, we were supplied with *Sugar* in the room of *Oil*, and with *Wheat* for a part of our *Oatmeal*, and were certainly gainers by the exchange. Sugar, I apprehend, is a very good antiscorbutic; whereas oil (such as the navy is usually supplied with), I am of opinion, has the contrary effect.

But the introduction of the most salutary articles, either as provisions or as medicines, will generally prove unsuccessful unless supported by certain regulations. On this principle, many years' experience, together with some hints I had from other intelligent officers, enabled me to lay a plan whereby all was to be governed.

The crew were at three watches, except upon some extraordinary occasions. By this means they were not so much exposed to the weather as if they had been at watch and watch; and they generally had dry clothes to shift themselves when they happened to get wet. Care was also taken to expose them as little to wet weather as possible.

Proper methods were used to keep their persons, hammocks, bedding, clothes, &c., constantly clean and dry. Equal care was taken to keep the ship clean and dry betwixt decks. Once or twice a week she was aired with fires; and when this could not be done, she was smoked with gunpowder mixed with vinegar or water. I had also, frequently, a fire made in an iron pot, at the bottom of the well, which was of great use in purifying the air in the lower parts of the ship. To this, and to cleanliness as well in the ship as amongst the people, too great attention cannot be paid; the least neglect occasions a putrid and disagreeable smell below, which nothing but fires will remove.

I was careful to take in water wherever it was to be got, even though we did not want it, because I look upon fresh water from the shore to be more wholesome than that which has been kept some time on board a ship. Of this essential article we were never at an allowance, but had always plenty for every necessary purpose. Navigators in general cannot expect to meet with such advantages in this respect as fell to my lot. The nature of our voyage carried us into very high latitudes. But the hardships and dangers inseparable from that situation were in some degree compensated for by the singular felicity we enjoyed of extracting inexhaustible sup-

plies of fresh water from an ocean strewed with
ice.

We came to few places where either the art of
man or the bounty of nature had not provided
some sort of refreshment or other, either in the
animal or vegetable way. It was my first care to
procure whatever of any kind could be met with,
by every means in my power, and to oblige our
people to make use thereof, both by my example
and by my authority; but the benefits arising from
refreshments of any kind soon became so obvious
that I had little occasion to recommend the one or
to exert the other.

It is with real satisfaction, and without claiming
any merit but that of attention to my duty, that
I can conclude this account with an observation
which facts enable me to make, that our having
discovered the possibility of preserving health
amongst a numerous ship's company, for such a
length of time, in such varieties of climate, and
amidst such continued hardships and fatigues, will
make this voyage remarkable in the opinion of
every benevolent person, when the dispute about a
Southern Continent shall have ceased to engage the
attention and to divide the judgment of philosophers.

## THE THIRD VOYAGE, 1776–1780

Another interesting geographical question had been re-discussed: that of the possibility of a "North-west Passage", that is, a navigable channel between the Atlantic and the Pacific, to the north of America, whereby vessels might be saved the tedious and unhealthy slow sailing across the tropical parts of the Atlantic. During the sixteenth and seventeenth centuries many attempts had been made to find such a passage from the Atlantic. It was now determined to attack the problem from the other side, and Cook volunteered to go in command of the expedition. Two ships were fitted out, his old vessel the *Resolution*, and the *Discovery*, of 300 tons, under Captain Clerke. Cook's instructions were to go through the Indian Ocean to the Pacific, to gather more information about the latter ocean and its islands as he passed through it, and then to try to find a passage to the Atlantic north of 65° north latitude.

The ships left Plymouth on July 11th, 1776, and, after calling at the Cape, passed through the Indian Ocean, south of 40° south, visiting the newly-discovered Kerguelen Land on the way. From Tasmania they went to New Zealand, and there learned the circumstances that led to the murder of some of the *Adventure's* crew in the previous voyage. They stayed in Queen Charlotte Sound from the 12th to the 25th of February, 1777, and then went north-east, and voyaged among the Pacific Islands near the parallel of 20° south, staying at the Friendly Islands from the end of April till the middle of July, and at the Society Islands till the beginning of December.

Then they sailed away north, to spend the northern summer

of 1778 in the search for the "North-west Passage". They fell in with the more westerly of the Sandwich Islands in January, 1778. Thence they bore away to the north-east, and reached the west coast of North America about 44° north on March 6th. The ships were overhauled in Nootka Sound, Vancouver Island, and then they followed the coast northwards, trying all likely places for the passage. At the beginning of July they entered Behring Sea, and on the 9th passed the most westerly point of North America, to which the name "Cape Prince of Wales" was given. They visited both sides of Behring Strait, and on August 12th entered the Arctic Circle. The rest of August was spent in vain attempts to find a way through the ice. Failing in this, Cook withdrew, to spend the winter in exploring the North Pacific, intending to renew the search for a passage in the following summer. In one of the Aleutian Islands they met some Russian traders, from whom they got some geographical information. Then, steering south, they came to the Sandwich Islands towards the end of November.

They spent the time till February 4th, 1779, at Owhyhee, the largest of the islands. Here they were received with the greatest kindness, and Captain Cook was treated by the priests and most of the people with what looked like adoration. The warrior chiefs, however, were less effusive in their friendship. But the death of a seaman, the great consumption of supplies, and the taking of the fence of a sacred place for fuel, all seemed to lessen the importance of the visitors in the eyes of the natives; and a plain intimation was given that the visit had lasted long enough. A few days after their departure, they had to return to replace a damaged mast, and their reception was distinctly unfriendly. Thefts, previously common, became more common and more serious, and, in an attempt to seize a chief as hostage for the return of a stolen boat, an attack was made by the natives, and Captain Cook was killed, on February 14th. His body was carried off, dismembered, and partly burned; but most of it was recovered and received seaman's burial.

The ships then left the Sandwich Islands, Captain Clerke taking command of the *Resolution*, and Lieutenant Gore of the *Discovery*. They spent May and part of June at St. Peter and St. Paul in Kamtschatka, where they were very kindly treated by the Russians, and then sailed through Behring Strait into the Arctic Ocean. During most of July they tried, with no success, to get through the ice, and then returned to St. Peter and St. Paul. Just before they reached it, Captain Clerke died of consumption, and was succeeded in command of the *Resolution* by Captain Gore, Lieutenant King taking command of the *Discovery*.

In October they began their homeward voyage, through the Indian and Atlantic Oceans, calling at Canton and Cape Town, and reached the Thames on October 4th, 1780.

The story of the murder of Captain Cook has received a curious explanation. It appears that the people of Hawaii at first took him to be one of their deities, who had long before left the island under a promise to return. Hence the divine honours paid to him. But, as already said, the death of one of the seamen, the heavy drain of supplies, and the taking of the sacred fence must have shown them their mistake, and they were glad to see him go away. When he unexpectedly returned a few days later, the people no longer had any special regard for him, thefts led to quarrels, and in a riot he was killed.

## 1. KERGUELEN'S LAND

December, 1776. My instructions directing me to examine the land recently discovered by Monsieur de Kerguelen, with a view to discover a good harbour, I proceeded in the search. [He found

Kerguelen's Land on December 24th.] At day-break in the morning of the 25th we weighed with a gentle breeze at west; and having wrought into the harbour to within a quarter of a mile of the sandy beach at its head, we anchored in eight fathoms of water, the bottom a fine dark sand. The *Discovery* did not get in till two o'clock in the afternoon; when Captain Clerke informed me that he had narrowly escaped being driven on the south point of the harbour, his anchor having started before they had time to shorten in the cable.

As soon as we had anchored I ordered all the boats to be hoisted out, the ship to be moored with a kedge anchor, and the water-casks to be got ready to send on shore. In the meantime I landed, to look for the most convenient spot where they might be filled, and to see what else the place afforded.

I found the shore in a manner covered with penguins and other birds and seals. These latter were not numerous, but so insensible of fear (which plainly indicated that they were unaccustomed to such visitors) that we killed as many as we chose, for the sake of their fat or blubber, to make oil for our lamps and other uses. Fresh water was in no less plenty than were birds, for every gully afforded a large stream. But not a single tree or shrub, nor the least sign of any, was to be discovered, and but very little herbage of any sort. The appearance, as we sailed into the harbour, had flattered us with the hope of meeting with something considerable growing here, as we observed the sides of many of the hills to be of a lively green. But I now found that this was occasioned by a single plant. Before I returned to my ship, I ascended the first ridge of rocks, which rise in a kind of amphitheatre above one another. I was in hopes, by this means, of obtaining a view of the country; but before I reached the top there came on so thick a fog that I could hardly find my way down again. In the evening we hauled the seine at the head of the harbour, but caught only half a dozen small fish. We had no better success next day, when we tried with hook and line. So that our only resource here for fresh provisions was in the birds, of which there was an inexhaustible store.

The morning of the 26th proved foggy with rain. However, we went to work to fill water, and to cut grass for our cattle, which we found in small spots near the head of the harbour. The rain which fell swelled all the rivulets to such a degree that the sides of the hills bounding the harbour seemed to be covered with a sheet of water. For the rain, as it fell, ran into the fissures and crags of the rocks that composed the interior parts of the hills, and was precipitated down their sides in prodigious torrents.

The people having wrought hard the two preceding days, and nearly completed our water, I allowed them the 27th as a day of rest, to celebrate Christmas. Upon this indulgence many of them went on shore, and made excursions in different directions into the country, which they found barren and desolate in the highest degree. In the evening one of them brought to me a quart bottle which he had found fastened with some wire to a projecting rock on the north side of the harbour.

[This contained a record of the visits of Kerguelen in 1772 and 1773. Cook added the record of his own visit.]

I put the parchment again into a bottle, together with a silver twopenny piece of 1772; and having covered the mouth of the bottle with a leaden cap, I placed it, the next morning, in a pile of stones, erected for the purpose, upon a little eminence on the north shore of the harbour, and near to the place where it was first found; in which position it cannot escape the notice of any European whom chance or design may bring into the port. Here I displayed the British flag, and named the place *Christmas Harbour*, from our having arrived in it on that festival.

Mr. Anderson, my surgeon, lost no opportunity,

during the short time we lay in Christmas Harbour, of searching the country in every direction. He afterwards communicated to me the observations he made on its natural productions, and I shall insert them here in his own words.

Perhaps no place hitherto discovered in either hemisphere under the same parallel of latitude affords so scanty a field for the naturalist as this barren spot. The verdure which appears when we are at a little distance from the shore would flatter one with the expectation of meeting with some herbage; but in this we were much deceived. For, on landing, we saw that this lively colour was occasioned by only one small plant, not much unlike some sorts of Saxifrage, which grows in large spreading tufts to a considerable way up the hills. It forms a surface of a pretty large texture, and grows on a kind of rotten turf, into which one sinks a foot or two at every step. This turf, dried, might in cases of necessity serve for fuel, and is the only thing we met here that could possibly be applied to this use.

There is another plant, plentifully enough scattered about the boggy declivities, which grows to near the height of two feet, and is not much unlike a small cabbage when it has shot into seeds. The leaves about the root are numerous, large, and rounded, narrower at the base, and ending in a small point. Those on the stalk are much smaller, oblong, and pointed. The stalks, which are three or four, all rise separately from the root, and run into long cylindrical heads, composed of small flowers. It has not only the appearance but the watery acrid taste of the antiscorbutic plants, and yet differs materially from the whole tribe, so that we looked upon it as a production entirely peculiar to the place. We ate it frequently raw, and found it almost like the New Zealand scurvy-grass. But it seemed to acquire a rank flavour by being boiled, which, however, some of our people did not perceive. At this time none of its seeds were ripe enough to be preserved and brought home.

Two other plants were found near the brooks and boggy places, which were eaten as salad, the one almost like garden cresses and very fiery, and the other very mild. A coarse grass, which we cut down for the cattle, grows pretty plentifully in a few small spots about the sides of the harbour, with a smaller sort which is rarer; and upon the flat ground a sort of goose-grass and another small plant much like it. In short, the whole catalogue of plants does not exceed sixteen or eighteen, including some sorts of moss and a beautiful species of lichen, which grows upon the rocks higher up than the rest of the vegetable productions. Nor is there even the least appearance of a shrub in the whole country.

Nature has been more bountiful in furnishing it with animals; though, strictly speaking, they are not inhabitants of the place, being all of the marine kind, and in general using the land only for breeding and for a resting-place.

The most considerable are seals, or, as we used to call them, sea-bears. These come ashore to rest or breed, but they were not very numerous, which is not to be wondered at, as it is known that these animals rather frequent out-rocks and little islands lying off coasts than bays or inlets. They were at this time shedding their hair, and so tame that we killed what number we chose.

No other quadruped, either of the sea or of the land kind, was seen; but a great number of birds, as ducks, petrels, albatrosses, shags, gulls, and sea-swallows. The ducks were about the size of a teal or widgeon. They were in tolerable plenty about the sides of the hills or even lower, and we killed a considerable number, which were good, and without the least fishy taste. Of the albatrosses none were found on shore except the gray one, which is commonly met with at sea in the higher southern latitudes. Once I saw one of these sitting in the cliff of a rock, but they were frequently flying about the harbour; and the common large sort, as well as the smaller with a black face, were seen farther out. Penguins form by far the greatest number of birds here, and are of three sorts. All the three sorts of penguins were so tame that we took as many as we pleased with our hands.

Another sort of white bird, flocks of which flew about the bay, is very singular, having the base of the bill covered with a horny crust. It is larger than a pigeon, with the bill black, and the feet white, made like those of the curlew. Some of our people put it in competition with the duck as food.

The hills are of a moderate height, yet many of their tops were covered with snow at this time, though answering to our June. Some of them have large quantities of stones irregularly heaped together at their foot or on their sides. The sides of others, which form steep cliffs towards the sea, are rent from the top downwards, and seem ready to fall off, having stones of a considerable size lying in the fissures. Some were of opinion that frost might be the cause of these fissures, which I shall not dispute; but how others of the appearances could be effected but by earthquakes, or some such severe shocks, I cannot say.

It appears that rain must be almost constant here, not only from the marks of large torrents having rushed down, but from the disposition of the country, which, even on the hills, is almost an entire bog or swamp, the ground sinking at every step.

## 2. THE NATIVES OF TASMANIA

[This race of people is now entirely extinct.]

January 28th, 1777.   In the afternoon we were agreeably surprised, at the place where we were cutting wood, with a visit from some of the natives, eight men and a boy.   They approached us from the woods without betraying any marks of fear, or rather with the greatest confidence imaginable, for none of them had any weapons, except one, who held in his hand a stick about two feet long and pointed at one end.

They were quite naked, and wore no ornaments, unless we consider as such, and as proof of their love of finery, some large punctures or ridges raised on different parts of their bodies, some in straight and others in curved lines.

They were of the common stature, but rather slender.   Their skin was black, and also their hair, which was as woolly as that of any native of New Guinea; but they were not distinguished by re- markably thick lios or flat noses.   On the contrary,

their features were far from being disagreeable.
They had pretty good eyes, and their teeth were
tolerably even, but very dirty. Most of them had
their hair and beards smeared with a red ointment,
and some had their faces also painted with the
same composition.

They received every present we made to them
without the least appearance of satisfaction. When
some bread was given, as soon as they understood
that it was to be eaten, they either returned it or
threw it away without even tasting it. They also
refused some fish, both raw and dressed, which we
offered them. But upon our giving some birds to
them they did not return these, and easily made
us comprehend that they were fond of such food.
I had brought two pigs ashore, with a view to
leaving them in the woods. The instant these
came within their reach, they seized them by the
ears, and were for carrying them off immediately,
with no other intention that we could perceive but
to kill them.

Being desirous of knowing the use of the stick
which one of our visitors carried in his hand, I
made signs to them to show me; and so far succeeded that one of them set up a piece of wood as
a mark and threw at it at the distance of about
twenty yards. But we had little reason to com-

mend his dexterity, for, after repeated trials, he was still wide of the mark. One of us, to show them how much superior our weapons were to theirs, then fired his musket at it, which alarmed them so much that, notwithstanding all we could do or say, they ran instantly into the woods. One of them was so frightened that he let drop an axe and two knives that had been given to him. From us, however, they went to the place where some of the *Discovery's* people were employed in taking water into their boat. The officer of that party, not knowing that they had paid us so friendly a visit, nor what their intent might be, fired a musket in the air, which sent them off with the greatest precipitation.

Some of the group wore, loose, round their necks, three or four folds of small cord made of the fur of some animal, and others of them had a slip of the kangaroo skin tied round their ankles. I gave to each of them a string of beads and a medal, which I thought they received with some satisfaction. They seemed to set no value on iron or on iron tools. They were even ignorant of the use of fish-hooks, if we may judge from their manner of looking at some of ours that we showed to them.

We cannot, however, suppose it to be possible that a people who inhabit a sea-coast, and who

seem to derive no part of their sustenance from
the productions of the ground, should not be acquainted with some mode of catching fish, though
we did not happen to see any of them thus employed, nor observe any canoe or vessel in which
they could go upon the water. Though they
absolutely rejected the sort of fish that was offered
them, it was evident that shell-fish, at least, made
a part of their food, from the many heaps of
mussel-shells we saw in different parts near the
shore, and about some deserted habitations near
the head of the bay. These were little sheds or
hovels built of sticks and covered with bark. We
could also perceive evident signs of their sometimes
taking up their abode in the trunks of large trees
which had been hollowed out by fire, most probably for this very purpose. In or near all these
habitations, and wherever there was a heap of
shells, there remained the marks of fire, an indubitable proof that they do not eat their food raw.

Several women and children made their appearance in the afternoon, and were introduced to
Lieutenant King by some of the men. He gave
presents to all of them of such trifles as he had
about him. These women wore kangaroo skins, in
the same shape as they came from the animal, tied
over the shoulder and round the waist. But its

only use seemed to be to support the children when carried on their backs; they were in other respects as naked as the men, and as black, and their bodies were marked with scars in the same manner. But in this they differed from the men, that, though their hair was of the same colour and texture, some of them had their heads completely shorn or shaved; in others this operation had been performed only on one side; while the rest of them had all the upper part of the head shorn close, leaving a circle of hair all round, somewhat like the tonsure of the Catholic ecclesiastics. Many of the children had fine features, and were thought pretty.

### 3. THE SANDWICH ISLANDS

We were seeing birds every day, sometimes in greater numbers than others, and several turtles. All these are looked upon as signs of the vicinity of land. In the morning of January 18th, 1778, an island made its appearance, and soon after we saw more land, entirely detached from the former. We had light airs and calms by turns, so that at sunset we were not less than nine or ten leagues from the nearest land. Our latitude was 21° 12′ N., and longitude 159° 19′ W.

January 19th. When we were about two leagues distant, we were in some doubt whether or no the land before us was inhabited; but this doubt was soon cleared up by our seeing some canoes coming off from the shore toward the ships. I immediately brought to, to give them time to join us. They had from three to six men each; and, on their approach, we were agreeably surprised to find that they spoke the language of Otaheite. It required but very little address to get them to come alongside; but no entreaties could prevail upon any of them to come on board. I tied some brass medals to a rope, and gave them to those in one of the canoes, who, in return, tied some small mackerel to the rope, as an equivalent. This was repeated; and some small nails, or bits of iron, which they valued more than any other article, were given them. For these they exchanged more fish and a sweet-potato; a sure sign that they had some notion of bartering, or, at least, of returning one present for another. They had nothing else in their canoes, except some large gourd-shells and a kind of fishing-net.

Seeing no signs of an anchoring-place at this eastern extreme of the island, I bore away to leeward, and ranged along the south-east side, at the distance of half a league from the shore. As soon as we made sail, the canoes left us; but others came off as we proceeded along the coast, bringing with them roasting pigs and some very fine potatoes, which they exchanged, as the others had done, for whatever was offered to them. Several small pigs were purchased for a sixpenny nail; so that we again found ourselves in a land of plenty, and that just at a time when the turtles that we had so fortunately procured at Christmas Island were nearly expended. We passed several villages, some seated near the sea, and others farther up the country. The inhabitants of all of them crowded to the shore, and collected themselves on the elevated places to view the ships.

January 20th. We stood in for the land, and were met by several canoes filled with people, some of whom took courage and ventured on board. In the course of my several voyages I never before met with the natives of any place so much astonished as these people were upon entering a ship. Their eyes were continually flying from object to object, the wildness of their looks and gestures fully expressing their entire ignorance about everything they saw, and strongly marking to us that, till now, they had never been visited by Europeans, nor been acquainted with any of our commodities, except iron, which, however, it was plain they had only heard of, or had known it in some small quantity, brought to them at some distant period.

M 738
"I NEVER BEFORE MET WITH NATIVES OF ANY PLACE SO MUCH
ASTONISHED AS THESE PEOPLE WERE UPON ENTERING A SHIP"

At first, on their entering the ship, they endeavoured to steal everything they came near, or rather to take it openly, as what we either should not resent, or not hinder. We soon convinced them of their mistake; and if they, after some time, became less active in appropriating to themselves whatever they took a fancy to, it was because they found that we kept a watchful eye over them.

At nine o'clock I sent three armed boats to look for a landing-place and for fresh water. About noon they came back, and the officer reported that he had seen a large pond behind a beach near one of the villages, which the natives told him contained fresh water; and that there was anchoring ground before it.

The ships being stationed, between three and four I went ashore with three armed boats and twelve marines, to examine the water, and to try the disposition of the inhabitants, several hundred of whom were assembled on a sandy beach before the village, behind which was a narrow valley, the bottom of which was occupied by the piece of water.

The very instant I leaped on shore, the collected body of the natives all fell flat upon their faces, and remained in that very humble posture till, by expressive signs, I prevailed upon them to rise.

They then brought me a great many small pigs, which they presented to me, with plantain trees, using much the same ceremonies that we had seen practised on such occasions at the Society and other islands; and a long prayer was spoken by a single person, in which others of the assembly sometimes joined. I expressed my acceptance of their proffered friendship by giving them, in return, such presents as I had brought with me from the ship for that purpose. When this introductory part of the business was finished, I stationed a guard upon the beach, and got some of the natives to conduct me to the water, which proved to be very good, and in a proper situation for our purpose. It was so considerable that it may be called a lake, and it extended farther up the country than we could see.

January 21st. As soon as we landed, a trade was set on foot for hogs and potatoes, which the people of the island gave us in exchange for nails and pieces of iron formed into something like chisels. We met with no obstruction in watering; on the contrary, the natives assisted our men in rolling the casks to and from the pool, and readily performed whatever we required. Everything thus going on to my satisfaction, and considering my presence on the spot as unnecessary, I made an excursion into the country, up the valley, accompanied by Mr. Anderson and Mr. Webber, the former of whom was as well qualified to describe with his pen, as the latter was to represent with his pencil, everything we might meet with worthy of observation.

A numerous train of natives followed us; and one of them, whom I had distinguished for his activity in keeping the rest in order, I made choice of as our guide. This man from time to time proclaimed our approach, and everyone whom we met fell prostrate upon the ground, and remained in that position till we had passed. This, as I afterwards understood, is the mode of paying their respect to their own great chiefs. As we ranged down the coast in the ships, we had observed at every village one or more elevated white objects, like pyramids, or rather obelisks; and one of these, which I guessed to be at least fifty feet high, was very conspicuous from the ship's anchoring station, and seemed to be at no great distance up this valley. To have a nearer inspection of it was the principal object of my walk.

Our guide perfectly understood that we wished to be conducted to it, but it happened to be so placed that we could not get at it, being separated from it by the pool of water. However, there

being another of the same kind within our reach,
about half a mile off, upon our side of the valley,
we set out to visit that. The moment we got to
it we saw that it stood in a burying-ground, the
resemblance of which, in many respects, to those
we were so well acquainted with in other islands of
this ocean, and particularly Tahiti, could not but
strike us. It was an oblong space of considerable
extent, surrounded by a wall of stone about four
feet high. The space inside was loosely paved with
smaller stones, and at one end of it stood what I
call the pyramid, which appeared evidently to be
an exact model of the larger one observed by us
from the ships. It was about four feet square at
the base, and about twenty feet high. The four
sides were composed of small poles interwoven with
twigs and branches, thus forming an indifferent
wicker-work, hollow or open within from bottom
to top. It seemed to be in a rather ruinous state,
but there were sufficent marks to show that it
had originally been covered with a thin, light, gray
cloth, which these people, it seems, consecrate to
religious purposes. Before the pyramid were a few
pieces of wood, carved into something like human
figures. On the farther side of the area stood a
house or shed about forty feet by ten feet. On the
farther side of this house, opposite the entrance,

stood two wooden images, cut out of one piece, with pedestals, in all about three feet high, neither very indifferently designed nor executed. These were said to be representatives of goddesses. On the head of one of them was a carved helmet, not unlike those worn by the ancient warriors, and on that of the other a cylindrical cap resembling the head-dress at Tahiti. In the middle of the house, and before the two images, was an oblong space, enclosed by a low edging of stone. This, on enquiry, we found was the grave of seven chiefs. On coming out of the house, just on one side of its entrance, we saw a small square place, and another still less, near it; and on our asking what these were, our guide immediately informed us that in the one was buried a man who had been sacrificed, and in the other a hog, which also had been made an offering to the divinity. At a little distance from these, near the middle of the enclosure, were three more of these square enclosed places. These, we were told, were the graves of three chiefs, and before them was an oblong enclosed space, of which our conductor told us, so explicitly that we could not mistake his meaning, that three human sacrifices had been buried there, that is, one at the funeral of each chief.

Our road to and from this burial-ground lay

through the plantations. The greatest part of the ground was quite flat, with ditches full of water intersecting different parts, and roads that seemed artificially raised to some height. The interspaces were in general planted with taro, which grows here with great strength, as the fields are sunk below the common level, so as to contain the water necessary to nourish the roots. On the drier spaces were several spots where the cloth-mulberry was planted, in regular rows, also growing vigorously, and kept very clean. The cocoa trees were not in so thriving a state, and were all low; but the plantain trees made a better appearance, though they were not large. The greatest part of the village stands near the beach, and consists of above sixty houses there, but perhaps about forty more stand scattered about, farther up the country toward the burying-place.

At sunset I brought everybody on board, having procured in the course of the day nine tons of water, and, by exchanges, chiefly for nails and pieces of iron, about seventy or eighty pigs, a few fowl, a quantity of potatoes, and a few plantains and taro roots. These people merited our best commendations in this commercial intercourse, never once attempting to cheat us, either ashore or alongside the ships.

## 4. THE COAST AND NATIVES OF NORTH AMERICA

March 11th, 1778. That part of the land which we were near [about 45° N.] is of moderate height, though in some places it rises higher within. It was diversified with a great many rising grounds and small hills, many of which were entirely covered with tall, straight trees, and others which were lower and grew in spots like coppices; but the interspaces and sides of many of the rising grounds were clear. The whole, though it might make an agreeable summer prospect, had now an uncomfortable appearance, as the bare grounds towards the coast were all covered with snow, which seemed to be of a considerable depth between the little hills and rising grounds, and in several places toward the sea might easily have been mistaken at a distance for white cliffs. The snow on the rising grounds was thinner spread, and farther inland there was no appearance of any; from whence we might conclude, perhaps, that what we saw toward the sea had all fallen during the night, which was colder than any we had experienced since our arrival on the coast, and we had sometimes a kind of sleet.

March 29th [about 50° N.]. The appearance of the country differed much from that of the parts we had before seen, being full of high mountains, whose summits were covered with snow. But the valleys between them, and the grounds on the sea-coast, high as well as low, were covered to a considerable breadth with high, straight trees, that formed a beautiful prospect, as of one vast forest.

We no sooner drew near the inlet of Nootka Sound than we found the coast to be inhabited, and three canoes came off to the ship. Having come pretty near us, a person in one of them stood up and made a long harangue, inviting us to land, as we guessed by his gestures. At the same time he kept strewing handfuls of feathers towards us, and some of his companions threw handfuls of a red dust or powder in the same manner. The person who played the orator wore the skin of some animal, and held in each hand something which rattled as he kept shaking it. After tiring himself with his repeated exhortations, of which we did not understand a word, he was quiet; and then others took it by turns to say something, though they acted their part neither so long nor with so much vehemence as the other. We observed that two or three had their hair quite strewed over with small white feathers, and others had large ones stuck into different parts of the head. After the tumultuous noise had ceased, they lay at a little distance from the ship, and conversed with each other in a very easy manner, nor did they seem to show the least surprise or distrust. Some of them got up now and then and said something after the manner of their first harangues, and one sang an agreeable air, with a degree of softness and melody that we could not have expected. One canoe was remarkable for a singular head, which had a bird's eye and bill of an enormous size painted on it; and a person who was in it, who seemed to be a chief, was no less remarkable for his uncommon appearance, having many feathers hanging from his head, and being painted in an extraordinary manner.

March 30th. A great many canoes filled with the natives were about the ships all day, and a trade commenced betwixt us and them which was carried on with the strictest honesty on both sides. The articles which they offered for sale were skins of various animals, such as bears, wolves, foxes, deer, racoons, polecats, martens, and in particular of the sea otters, which are found at the islands east of Kamtschatka. Besides the skins in their natural shape, they also brought garments made of them, and another sort of clothing made of the bark of a tree or some plant like hemp; weapons, such as bows, arrows, and spears; fish-hooks and instruments of various kinds; wooden vizors of

many different monstrous figures; a sort of woollen
stuff or blanketing; bags filled with red ochre;
pieces of carved work; beads; and several other
little ornaments of brass and iron shaped like a
horse-shoe, which they hang at their noses; and
several chisels or pieces of iron fixed to handles.
From their possessing these metals we could infer
that they had either been visited before by some
civilized nation, or had connection with tribes on
their continent who had communication with them.
But the most extraordinary of all the articles which
they brought to the ships for sale were human
skulls and hands not yet quite stripped of the
flesh, which they made our people plainly understand they had eaten; and, indeed, some of them
had evident marks that they had been upon the
fire.   For the various articles which they brought
they took in exchange knives, chisels, pieces of
iron and tin, nails, looking-glasses, buttons, or any
kind of metal.   Glass beads they were not fond
of, and cloth of every sort they rejected.

A considerable number of the natives visited us
daily, and every now and then we saw new faces.
On their first coming they generally went through
a singular mode of introducing themselves.   They
would paddle with all their strength quite round
both ships, a chief or other principal person in the

canoe standing up with a spear or some other weapon in his hand, and speaking all the time. Sometimes the orator of the canoe would have his face covered with a mask representing either a human visage or that of some animal, and, instead of a weapon, would hold a rattle in his hand. After making this circuit round the ships, they would come alongside, and begin to trade without further ceremony. Very often, indeed, they would first give us a song, in which all in the canoe joined, with a very pleasing harmony.

## 5. THE CHUKCHIS OF NORTH-EAST ASIA

We perceived on the shore a village, and some people, whom the sight of the ships had thrown into confusion or fear. We could plainly see persons running up the country with burdens upon their backs. At these habitations I proposed to land, and, accordingly, went with three armed boats, accompanied by some of the officers. About thirty or forty men, each armed with a spear, a bow, and arrows, stood drawn up on a rising ground close by the village. As we drew near, three of them came down toward the shore, and were so polite as to take off their caps and to make us low bows. [This they had learned from Russian traders.] We returned the civility, but this did

not inspire them with sufficient confidence to wait
for our landing; for the moment we put the boats
ashore, they retired. I followed them alone, without anything in my hand, and by signs and
gestures prevailed on them to stop and to receive
some trifling presents. In return for these they
gave me two fox-skins and a couple of sea-horse
teeth.

They seemed very fearful and cautious, expressing their desire by signs that no more of our
people should come up. On my laying my hand
on the shoulder of one of them, he started back
several paces. In proportion as I advanced, they
retreated backward, always in the attitude of being
ready to make use of their spears, while those on
the rising ground stood ready to support them
with their arrows. Insensibly, myself and two or
three of my companions got in amongst them. A
few beads distributed to those about us created a
kind of confidence, so that they were not alarmed
when a few more of our people joined us; and by
degrees a sort of traffic between us commenced.
In exchange for knives, beads, and tobacco, they
gave us some of their clothing and a few arrows.
But nothing we had to offer could induce them to
part with a spear or a bow.

The arrows were pointed either with bone or

with stone, but very few of them had barbs, and
some had a round blunt point. What use these
may be applied to I cannot say, unless it be to
kill small animals without damaging the skin.
The spears were of iron or steel, and no little pains
had been taken to ornament them with carving,
and inlayings of brass and of a white metal. A
leathern quiver, slung over the left shoulder, contained arrows; and some of these quivers were
extremely beautiful, being made of red leather, on
which was very neat embroidery and other ornaments.

All the Americans we had seen were rather low
of stature, with round chubby faces and high
cheek-bones. The people we were now amongst
had long visages, and were stout and well made.
They seemed to be picked men, and rather under
than above the middle age. All of them had
their ears bored, and some had glass beads hanging to them.

Their clothing consisted of a cap, a frock, a pair
of breeches, a pair of boots, and a pair of gloves,
all made of leather, or of the skins of deer, dogs,
seals, &c., and extremely well dressed, some with
the hair or fur on, but others without it. The
caps were made to fit the head very close; and
besides these caps, which most of them wore, we

got from them some hoods, made of skins of dogs, that were large enough to cover both head and shoulders. Their hair seemed to be black, but their heads were either shaved, or the hair cut close off, and none of them wore any beard.

We found the village composed of both their summer and their winter habitations. The latter are exactly like a vault, the floor of which is sunk a little below the surface of the earth. One of them which I examined was of an oval form, about twenty feet long and twelve or more high. The framing was composed of wood and the ribs of whales, and bound together with smaller material of the same sort. Over this framing is laid a covering of strong, coarse grass; and that again is covered with earth; so that on the outside the house looks like a little hillock, supported by a wall of stone three or four feet high, which is built round the two sides and one end. At the other end the earth is raised sloping, to walk up to the entrance, which is by a hole in the top of the roof over that end.

The summer huts were pretty large and circular, being brought to a point at the top. The framing was of slight poles and bones, covered with the skins of sea-animals. I examined the inside of one. There was a fireplace just within the door, where lay a few wooden vessels, all very dirty. Their bed places were close to the side, and took up about half the circuit. The bed and bedding were of deer-skins, and most of them were dry and clean.

About the habitations were erected several stages, ten or twelve feet high. They were wholly composed of bones, and seemed intended for drying their fish and skins, which were thus placed beyond the reach of their dogs, of which they had a great many. These dogs are of the fox kind, rather large, and of different colours, with long, soft hair, like wool. They are probably used for drawing their sledges in winter. Sledges they have, as I saw a good many laid up in one of the winter huts. It is also not improbable that dogs may constitute a part of their food. Several lay dead that had been killed that morning.

### 6. ICY CAPE AND THE ARCTIC OCEAN, 1778

August 17th, 1778. Some time before noon we perceived a brightness in the northern horizon like that reflected from ice, commonly called the blink. It was little noticed, from a supposition that it was improbable we should meet with ice so soon. And yet the sharpness of the air and gloominess of the weather for two or three days past seemed to indicate some sudden changes. About an hour after, the sight of a large field of ice left us no longer in doubt about the cause of the brightness of the horizon. At half-past two we tacked, close to the edge of the ice, in twenty-two fathoms of water, being then in the latitude of 70° 41', not being able to stand on any farther. For the ice was quite impenetrable, and extended from w. by s. to E. by N. as far as the eye could reach. Here were abundance of sea-horses, some in the water, but more upon the ice.

On the 18th at noon our latitude was 70° 44', and we were near five leagues farther to the eastward. We were at this time close to the edge of the ice, which was as compact as a wall, and seemed ten or twelve feet high at least. But farther north it appeared much higher. Its surface was extremely rugged, and here and there we saw upon it pools of water.

We now stood to the southward, and, after running six leagues, shoaled the water to seven fathoms, but it soon deepened to nine fathoms. At this time the weather, which had been hazy, clearing up a little, we saw land extending from s. to s.e. by E., about three or four miles distant. The eastern extreme forms a point which was much encumbered with ice, for which reason it obtained the name of *Icy Cape*. The other extreme of the land was lost in the horizon, so that there can be no doubt of its being a continuation of the American continent.

Our situation was now more and more critical. We were in shoal water, upon a lee shore, and the main body of the ice to windward, driving down upon us. It was evident that if we remained much longer between it and the land it would force us ashore, unless it should happen to take the ground before us. It seemed nearly to join the land to leeward, and the only direction that was open was to the s.w. After making a short board to the northward, I made the signal to the *Discovery* to tack, and tacked myself at the same time.

In the morning of the 19th we had a good deal of drift-ice about us, and the main ice was about two leagues to the north. At half-past one we got in with the edge of it. It was not so compact as that which we had seen to the northward, but it was too close, and in too large pieces, to attempt forcing the ships through it.

On the ice lay a prodigious number of sea-horses, and, as we were in want of fresh provisions, the boats of each ship were sent to get some. By seven o'clock in the evening we had received on board the *Resolution* nine of these animals. We lived upon them as long as they lasted, and there were few on board that did not prefer them to our salt meat.

The fat at first is as sweet as marrow, but in a few days it grows rancid, unless it be salted. The lean flesh is coarse and black, and has a rather strong taste, but the heart is nearly as well tasted as that of a bullock. The fat when melted yields a good deal of oil, which burns very well in lamps; and their hides, which are very thick, were very useful about our rigging. The teeth or tusks of most of them were at this time very small; even some of the largest and oldest of these animals had them not exceeding six inches in length.

They lie, in herds of many hundreds, upon the ice, huddling one over the other like swine, and roar or bray very loud, so that in the night or in foggy weather they gave us notice of the vicinity of the ice before we could see it. We never found the whole herd asleep, some being always upon the watch. On the approach of the boat these would wake those next to them, and, the alarm being thus gradually communicated, the whole herd would be awake presently. But they were seldom in a hurry to get away till after they had been once fired at. Then they would tumble one over the other into the sea in the utmost confusion. And if we did not, at the first discharge, kill those we fired at, we generally lost them, though mortally wounded. They did not appear to us to be that dangerous animal some authors have described, not even when attacked. They are rather more so to appearance than in reality. Vast numbers of them would follow and come close up to the boats. But the flash of a musket in the pan, or even the bare pointing of one at them, would send them down in an instant. The female will defend the young one to the very last, and at the expense of her own life, whether in the water or upon the ice. Nor will the young one quit the dam though she be dead; so that, if you kill the one, you are sure of the other. The dam, when in the water, holds the young one between her fore-fins.

August 27th. It must not be understood that I supposed any part of this ice which we had seen to be fixed; on the contrary, I am well assured that the whole was a movable mass. Having but little wind, I went with the boats to examine the state of the ice. I found it consisting of loose pieces of various extent, and so close together that I could hardly enter the outer edge with a boat, and it was as impossible for the ships to enter it as if it had been so many rocks. I took particular notice that it was all pure transparent ice, except the upper surface, which was a little porous. It appeared to be entirely composed of frozen snow, and to have been all formed at sea. The pieces of ice that formed the outer edge of the field were from forty or fifty yards in extent to four or five, and I judged that the larger pieces reached thirty feet or more under the surface of the water. It appeared to me very improbable that this ice could have been the production of the preceding winter alone. I should suppose it rather to have been the production of a great many winters. Nor was it less improbable, according to my judgment, that the little that remained of the summer could destroy the tenth part of what now subsisted of this mass; for the sun had now exerted upon it the full influence of his rays. Indeed, I am of opinion that the sun contributes very little toward reducing these great masses. For although that luminary is a great while above the horizon, it seldom shines out for more than a few hours at a time, and often is not seen for several days in succession. It is the wind, or rather the waves raised by the wind, that brings down the bulk of these enormous masses, by grinding one piece against another, and by undermining and washing away those parts that lie exposed to the surge of the sea. This was evident from our observing that the upper surface of many pieces had been partly washed away, while the base or under part remained firm for several fathoms round that which appeared above water, exactly like a shoal round an elevated rock. We measured the depth of water upon one, and found it to be fifteen feet; so that the ships might have sailed over it.

August 29th. The season was now so far advanced, and the time when the frost is expected to set in so near at hand, that I did not consider it consistent with prudence to make any further attempts to find a passage into the Atlantic this year, in any direction, so little was the prospect of succeeding. My attention was now directed toward finding out some place where we might supply ourselves with wood and water, and so spend the winter as to be in a condition to return to the north in farther search of a passage the ensuing summer.

## 7. CEREMONIOUS RECEPTION OF CAPTAIN COOK IN HAWAII

[This is narrated by Captain King.]

January 17th, 1779. There was brought on board the *Resolution* a chief named Koah, who, we were told, was a priest, and had been in his youth a distinguished warrior. He was a little, old man, of an emaciated figure; his eyes were exceedingly sore and red, and his body was covered with a white leprous scurf. Being led into the cabin, he approached Captain Cook with great veneration, and threw over his shoulders a piece of red cloth, which he had brought along with him. Then, stepping a few paces back, he made an offering of a small pig, which he held in his hand, while he pronounced a discourse that lasted for a considerable time. This ceremony was frequently repeated during our stay at Owhyhee, and appeared to us, from many circumstances, to be a sort of religious adoration. Their idols we found always arrayed with red cloth, in the same manner as was Captain Cook; and a small pig was their usual offering to their deities. Their speeches, or prayers, were uttered, too, with a readiness and volubility that indicated them to be according to some formulary.

When this ceremony was over, Koah dined with Captain Cook, eating plentifully of what was set before him; but, like the rest of the inhabitants of the islands in these seas, could scarcely be prevailed on to taste a second time of wine or spirits.

In the evening Captain Cook, attended by Mr. Bayly and myself, accompanied Koah on shore. We landed at the beach, and were received by four men who carried wands tipped with dog's hair, and marched before us, pronouncing with a loud voice a short sentence, in which we could distinguish only the word "Orono", the name by which Captain Cook generally went amongst the natives of Owhyhee, and which they sometimes applied to an invisible being, who, they said, lived in the heavens. The crowd, which had been collected on the shore, retired at our approach, and not a person was to be seen, except a few lying prostrate on the ground near the huts of the adjoining village.

Before I proceed to relate the adoration that was paid to Captain Cook, and the peculiar ceremonies with which he was received on this fatal island, it will be necessary to describe the Morai, or sacred place, which was situated on the south side of the beach at the village of Kakooa. It was a square, solid pile of stones, about forty yards long, twenty broad, and fourteen in height. The top was flat and well paved, and surrounded by a wooden rail on which were fixed the skulls of the captives sacrificed on the death of their chiefs. In the centre of the area stood a ruinous old building of wood, connected with the rail on each side by a stone wall, which divided the whole space into two parts. On the side next the country were five poles, upward of twenty feet high, supporting an irregular kind of scaffold; on the opposite side, toward the sea, stood two small houses, with a covered communication.

We were conducted by Koah to the top of this pile by an easy ascent, leading from the beach to the N.W. corner of the area. At the entrance we saw two large wooden images, with features violently distorted, and a long piece of carved wood, of a conical form inverted, rising from the top of their heads; the rest was without form, and wrapped round with red cloth. We were here met by a tall young man with a long beard, who presented Captain Cook to the images; and after chanting a kind of hymn, in which he was joined by Koah, they led us to that end of the Morai where the five poles were fixed. At the foot of them were twelve images ranged in a semicircular form, and before the middle figure stood a high stand, on which lay a putrid pig, and under it pieces of sugar-cane, cocoa-nuts, bread-fruit, plantains, and sweet-potatoes. Koah, having placed the captain under this stand, took down the hog, and held it toward him; and, after having a second time addressed him in a long speech, pronounced with much vehemence and rapidity, he let it fall on the ground, and led him to the scaffolding, which they began to climb together, not without great risk of falling.   At this time we saw, coming in solemn procession, at the entrance of the top of the Morai, ten men carrying a live hog and a large piece of red cloth.   Being advanced a few paces, they stopped and prostrated themselves; and Kaireekeea, the young man afore-mentioned, went to them, and receiving the cloth, carried it to Koah, who wrapped it round the captain, and afterward offered him the hog, which was brought by Kaireekeea with the same ceremony.

Whilst Captain Cook was aloft in this awkward situation, swathed round with red cloth, and with difficulty keeping his hold amongst the pieces of rotten scaffolding, Kaireekeea and Koah began their office, chanting sometimes in concert and sometimes alternately.   This lasted a considerable time, till at length Koah let the hog drop, and he and the captain descended together.   He then led him to the images before-mentioned, and having said something to each in a sneering tone, snapping his fingers at them as he passed, he brought him to that in the centre, which, from its being covered with red cloth, appeared to be in greater estimation than the rest.   Before this figure he prostrated himself, and kissed it, desiring Captain Cook to do the same, who suffered himself to be directed by Koah throughout the whole of this ceremony.

We were now led back into the other division of the Morai, where there was a space ten or twelve feet square sunk about three feet below the level of the area. Into this we descended, and Captain Cook was seated between two wooden idols, Koah supporting one of his arms, while I was desired to support the other. At this time arrived a second procession of natives, carrying a baked hog and a pudding, some bread-fruit, cocoa-nuts, and other vegetables. When they approached us Kaireekeea put himself at their head, and, presenting the pig to Captain Cook in the usual manner, began the same kind of chant as before, his companions making regular responses. We observed that after every response their parts became gradually shorter, till, towards the close, Kaireekeea's consisted of only two or three words, which the rest answered with the word "Orono".

When this offering was concluded, which lasted a quarter of an hour, the natives sat down fronting us, and began to cut up the baked hog, to peel the vegetables, and break the cocoa-nuts, while others employed themselves in preparing drink. Kaireekeea then took part of the kernel of a cocoa-nut, which he chewed, and, wrapping it in a piece of cloth, rubbed with it the captain's face, head, hands, arms, and shoulders. The drink was then handed round, and after we had tasted it, Koah and another chief named Pareea began to pull the flesh of the hog in pieces, and to put it into our mouths. I had no great objection to being fed by Pareea, who was very cleanly in his person; but Captain Cook, who was served by Koah, could not swallow a morsel; and his reluctance, as may be supposed, was not diminished when the old man, according to his own mode of civility, had chewed it for him.

When this last ceremony was finished, which Captain Cook put an end to as soon as he decently could, we quitted the Morai, after distributing among the people some pieces of iron and other trifles, with which they seemed highly gratified. The men with wands conducted us to the boats, repeating the same words as before. The people again retired, and the few that remained prostrated themselves as we passed along the shore. We immediately went on board, our minds full of what we had seen, and extremely well satisfied with the good disposition of our new friends. The meaning of the various ceremonies with which we had been received, and which, on account of their novelty and singularity, have been related at length, can only be the subject of conjectures, and those uncertain and partial. They were, however, without doubt, expressive of high respect on the part of

the natives; and, as far as related to the person of
Captain Cook, they seemed approaching to adoration.

## 8. THE SANDWICH ISLANDERS

The inhabitants of the Sandwich Islands are
undoubtedly of the same race with those of New
Zealand, the Society and Friendly Islands, Easter
Island, and the Marquesas; a race that possesses,
without any intermixture, all the known lands
between the latitudes of 47° s. and 20° N., and
between the longitudes of 184° and 260° E. [*i.e.*
176° and 100° w.].

The natives of these islands are, in general,
above the middle size, and well made; they walk
very gracefully, run nimbly, and are capable of
bearing great fatigue; though, upon the whole, the
men are somewhat inferior, in point of strength
and activity, to the Friendly Islanders, and the
women less delicately limbed than those of Otaheite.
Their complexion is rather darker than that of the
Otaheiteans, and they are not altogether so handsome a people.

Notwithstanding the irreparable loss we suffered
from the sudden resentment and violence of these
people, yet, in justice to their general conduct, it
must be acknowledged that they are of the most

mild and affectionate disposition, equally remote from the extreme levity and fickleness of the Otaheiteans and the distant gravity and reserve of the inhabitants of the Friendly Islands. The women who had children were remarkable for their tender and constant attention to them, and the men would often lend their assistance in those domestic offices with a willingness that does credit to their feelings.

It must, however, be observed that they fall very short of the other islanders in that best test of civilization, the respect paid to the women. Here they are not only deprived of the privilege of eating with the men, but the best sorts of food are *tabooed* or forbidden to them. They are not allowed to eat pork, turtle, several kinds of fish, and some species of the plantains; and we were told that a poor girl got a terrible beating for having eaten, on board our ship, one of these interdicted articles. In their domestic life they appear to live almost entirely by themselves, and though we did not observe any instances of personal ill-treatment, yet it was evident that they had little regard or attention paid them.

The dress of the men generally consists only of a piece of thick cloth about ten or twelve inches broad, which they pass between the legs and tie round the waist. This is the common dress of all ranks of the people. Their mats, some of which are beautifully manufactured, are of various sizes, but mostly about five feet long and four broad. These they throw over their shoulders and bring forward; but they are seldom used except in time of war, for which purpose they seem better adapted than for ordinary use, being of a thick and cumbersome texture, and capable of breaking the blow of a stone or any blunt weapon. Their feet are generally bare, except when they have occasion to travel over the volcanic rocks, when they secure them with a sort of sandal made of cords twisted from the fibres of the cocoa-nut. Such is the ordinary dress of these islanders; but they have another, appropriated to their chiefs, and used on ceremonious occasions, consisting of a feathered cloak and helmet, which, in point of beauty and magnificence, is perhaps nearly equal to that of any nation in the world. These cloaks are nearly of the size and shape of the short cloaks worn by the women in England, and by the men in Spain, reaching to the middle of the back and tied loosely before. The ground of them is a net-work, upon which the most beautiful red and yellow feathers are so closely fixed that the surface might be compared to the thickest and richest velvet, which they resemble both as to the feel and the glossy appearance. The manner of varying the mixture is very different, some having triangular spaces of red and yellow alternately, others a kind of crescent, and some that were entirely red had a broad yellow border, which made them appear, at some distance, exactly like a scarlet cloak edged with gold lace. The brilliant colours of the feathers in those that were new added not a little to their fine appearance; and we found that they were in high estimation with their owners, for they would not, at first, part with any one of them for anything that we offered, asking no less a price than a musket. The cap is made almost exactly like a helmet, with the middle part, or crest, sometimes of a hand's-breadth; and it fits very close upon the head, having notches to admit the ears. It is a frame of twigs and osiers, covered with a net-work, into which are wrought feathers, in the same manner as upon the cloaks, though rather closer and less diversified, the greater part being red, with some black, yellow, or green stripes on the sides, following the curved direction of the crest.

Swimming is not only a necessary art, in which both the men and the women are more expert than any people we had hitherto seen, but a favourite

diversion amongst them.   One particular mode in
which they sometimes amused themselves appeared
to us most perilous and extraordinary, and well de-
serving a distinct relation.   The surf, which breaks
on the coast round the bay, extends to a distance
of about one hundred and fifty yards, within which
space the surges of the sea, accumulating from the
shallowness of the water, are dashed against the
beach with prodigious violence.   Whenever, from
stormy weather or any extraordinary swell at sea,
the impetuosity of the surf is increased to its
utmost height, they choose that time for this amusement.   Twenty or thirty of the natives, taking
each a long narrow board, rounded at the ends,
set out together from the shore.   The first wave
they meet they plunge under, and, suffering it
to roll over them, rise again beyond it, and make
the best of their way, by swimming, out into the
sea.   The second wave is encountered in the same
manner as the first, and so on.   As soon as they
have gained, by these repeated efforts, the smooth
water beyond the surf, they lay themselves at
length, each upon his board, and prepare for their
return.   As the surf consists of a number of waves,
of which every third is remarked to be always much
larger than the others, and to flow higher on the
shore, the rest breaking in the intermediate space,

their first object is to place themselves on the summit of the largest surge, by which they are driven along with amazing rapidity toward the shore. If by mistake they should place themselves on one of the smaller waves, which breaks before they reach the land, or should not be able to keep their planks in a proper direction on the top of the swell, they are left exposed to the fury of the next, and, to avoid it, are obliged again to dive, and regain the place from which they set out. Those who succeed in their object of reaching the shore have still the greatest danger to encounter. The coast being guarded by a chain of rocks, with, here and there, a small opening between them, they are obliged to steer their boards through one of these, or, in case of failure, to quit them, before they reach the rocks, and, plunging under the wave, make the best of their way back again. This is reckoned very disgraceful, and is also attended with the loss of the board, which I have often seen dashed to pieces at the moment the islander quitted it. The boldness and address with which we saw them perform these difficult and dangerous manœuvres was altogether astonishing, and is scarcely to be credited.

An accident, of which I was a near spectator, shows at how early a period they are so far familiarised to the water as both to lose all fears of it and to set its dangers at defiance. A canoe being overset, in which was a woman with her children, one of them, an infant, who, I am convinced, was not more than four years old, seemed highly delighted with what had happened, swimming about at its ease, and playing a hundred tricks, till the canoe was put to rights again.

### 9. THE DEATH OF CAPTAIN COOK

[This is related by Captain King.]

February 14th, 1779. I was informed that the cutter of the *Discovery* had been stolen during the night from the buoy where it was moored. It had been Captain Cook's usual practice, whenever anything of consequence was lost at any of the islands in this ocean, to get the king or some of the principal chiefs on board, and to keep them as hostages till it was restored. This method, which had been always attended with success, he meant to pursue on the present occasion; and, at the same time, had given orders to stop all the canoes that should attempt to leave the bay, with an intention of seizing and destroying them, if he could not recover the cutter by peaceable means.

It was between seven and eight o'clock when we quitted the ship together, Captain Cook in the pinnace, having Mr. Phillips and nine marines with him, and myself in the small boat. Captain Cook went toward Kowrowa where the king resided, and I went to the beach. Captain Cook immediately marched into the village, where he was received with the usual marks of respect, the people prostrating themselves before him, and bringing their accustomed offerings of small hogs. Finding that there was no suspicion of his design, his next step was to enquire for Terreeoboo, the king, and the two boys, his sons, who had been his constant guests on board the *Resolution*. In a short time the boys returned along with the natives who had been sent in search of them, and immediately led Captain Cook to the house where the king had slept. They found the old man just awoke from sleep; and, after a short conversation about the loss of the cutter, from which Captain Cook was convinced that he was in no wise privy to it, he invited him to return in the boat and spend the day on board the *Resolution*. To this proposal the king readily consented, and immediately got up to accompany him.

Things were in this prosperous train, the two boys being already in the pinnace and the rest of the party having advanced near the water-side, when an elderly woman called Kanee-kabareea, the mother of the boys and one of the king's favourite wives, came after him, and with many tears and entreaties besought him not to go on board. At the same time two chiefs, who came along with her, laid hold of him, and, insisting that he should go no farther, forced him to sit down. The natives, who were collecting in prodigious numbers along the shore, and had probably been alarmed at the firing of the great guns at some escaping canoes, and the appearance of hostility in the bay, began to throng round Captain Cook and the king. In this situation the lieutenant of marines, observing that his men were huddled close together in the crowd and thus incapable of using their arms if any occasion should require it, proposed to the captain to draw them up along the rocks close to the water's edge; and, the crowd readily making way for them to pass, they were drawn up in a line, at the distance of about thirty yards from the place where the king was sitting.

All this time the old king remained on the ground, with the strongest marks of terror and dejection in his countenance, Captain Cook, not willing to abandon the object for which he had come on shore, continuing to urge him, in the most pressing manner, to proceed; whilst, on the other hand, whenever the king appeared inclined to

follow him, the chiefs who stood round him inter-
posed, at first with prayers and entreaties, but
afterward having recourse to force and violence,
and insisted on his staying where he was.   Captain
Cook therefore, finding that the alarm had spread
too generally, and that it was in vain to think any
longer of getting him off without bloodshed, at last
gave up the point, observing to Mr. Phillips that it
would be impossible to compel him to go on board
without the risk of killing a great number of the
inhabitants.

Though the enterprise that had carried Captain
Cook on shore had failed and was abandoned, yet
his person did not appear to have been in the least
danger, till an accident happened which gave a
fatal turn to the affair.   The boats which had been
stationed across the bay, having fired at some
canoes that were attempting to get out, unfortu-
nately had killed a chief of the first rank.   The
news of his death arrived at the village where Captain Cook was just as he had left the king and was
walking slowly toward the shore.   The ferment it
occasioned was very conspicuous; the women and
children were immediately sent off; and the men
put on their war-mats, and armed themselves with
spears and stones.   One of the natives, having in
his hands a stone and a long iron spike, came up

to the captain, flourishing his weapon by way of defiance, and threatening to throw the stone. The captain desired him to desist; but, the man persisting in his insolence, he was at length provoked to fire a load of small-shot. The man having his mat on, which the shot were not able to penetrate, this had no other effect than to irritate and encourage them. Several stones were thrown at the marines; and one of the chiefs attempted to stab Mr. Phillips with his spear, but failed in the attempt, and received from him a blow with the butt end of his musket. Captain Cook now fired his second barrel, loaded with ball, and killed one of the foremost of the natives. A general attack with stones immediately followed, which was answered by a discharge of musketry from the marines and the people in the boats. The islanders, contrary to the expectations of everyone, stood the fire with great firmness, and before the marines had time to reload, they broke upon them with dreadful shouts and yells. What followed was a scene of the utmost horror and confusion.

Four of the marines were cut off amongst the rocks in the retreat, and fell a sacrifice to the fury of the enemy; three more were dangerously wounded; and the lieutenant, who had received a stab between the shoulders with a spear, having

THE FATAL FIGHT WITH THE NATIVES OF OWHYHEE

fortunately reserved his fire, shot the man who had wounded him just as he was going to repeat his blow. Our unfortunate commander, the last time he was seen distinctly, was standing at the water's edge, and calling out to the boats to cease firing and to pull in. If it be true, as some of those who were present have imagined, that the marines and boatmen had fired without his orders, and that he was desirous of preventing any further bloodshed, it is not improbable that his humanity on this occasion proved fatal to him. For it was remarked that whilst he faced the multitude none of them offered him any violence, but that, having turned about to give his orders to the boats, he was stabbed in the back, and fell with his face into the water. On seeing him fall, the islanders set up a great shout, and his body was immediately dragged on shore and surrounded by the enemy, who, snatching the dagger out of each other's hands, showed a savage eagerness to have a share in his destruction.

Thus fell our great and excellent commander. After a life of so much distinguished and successful enterprise, his death, as far as regards himself, cannot be reckoned premature, since he lived to finish the great work for which he seems to have been designed; and was rather removed from the enjoyment, than cut off from the acquisition, of glory. How sincerely his loss was felt and lamented by those who had so long found their general security in his skill and conduct, and every consolation, under their hardships, in his tenderness and humanity, it is neither necessary nor possible for me to describe; much less shall I attempt to paint the horror with which we were struck, and the universal dejection and dismay which followed so dreadful and unexpected a calamity. The reader will not be displeased to turn from so sad a scene to the contemplation of his character and virtues, whilst I am paying my last tribute to the memory of a dear and honoured friend.

The earliest habits of his life, the course of his services, and the constant application of his mind, all conspired to fit him for the prosecution of discoveries in the less known parts of the sea, and gave him a degree of professional knowledge which can fall to the lot of very few. The constitution of his body was robust, inured to labour, and capable of undergoing the severest hardships. His stomach bore, without difficulty, the coarsest and most ungrateful food. Indeed, temperance in him was scarcely a virtue, so great was the indifference with which he submitted to every kind of self-denial. The qualities of his mind were of the same hardy, vigorous kind with those of his body. His understanding was strong and perspicacious. His judgment, in whatever related to the services he was engaged in, quick and sure. His designs were bold and manly; and, both in the conception and in the mode of execution, bore evident marks of a great original genius. His courage was cool and determined, and accompanied with an admirable presence of mind in the moment of danger. His manners were plain and unaffected. His temper might perhaps have been justly blamed as subject to hastiness and passion, had not these been disarmed by a disposition the most benevolent and humane.

Such were the outlines of Captain Cook's character; but its most distinguishing feature was that unremitting perseverance in the pursuit of his object, which was not only superior to the opposition of dangers and the pressure of hardships, but even exempt from the want of ordinary relaxation. During the long and tedious voyages in which he was engaged, his eagerness and activity were never in the least abated. No incidental temptation could detain him for a moment; even those intervals of recreation, which sometimes unavoidably occurred, and were looked for by us with a longing that persons who have experienced the fatigues of service will readily excuse, were submitted to by him with a certain impatience, whenever they could not be employed in making further provision for the more effectual prosecution of his designs.

Perhaps no science ever received greater additions from the labours of a single man than geography has done from those of Captain Cook. As a navigator his services were not perhaps less splendid, certainly not less important and meritorious. The method which he discovered and so successfully pursued of preserving the health of seamen forms a new era in navigation, and will transmit his name to future ages amongst the friends and benefactors of mankind.

## 10. THE DEATH OF CAPTAIN CLERKE

On the 22nd of August, 1779, at nine o'clock in the morning, departed this life Captain Charles Clerke, in the thirty-eighth year of his age. He died of a consumption, which had evidently commenced before he left England, and of which he had lingered during the whole voyage. His very gradual decay had long made him a melancholy object to his friends; yet the equanimity with which he bore it, the constant flow of good spirits, which continued to the last hour, and a cheerful resignation to his fate afforded them some consolation. It was impossible not to feel a more than common degree of compassion for a person whose life had been a continued scene of those difficulties and hardships to which a seaman's occupation is subject, and under which he at last sank.

He was brought up to the navy from his earliest youth, and had been in several actions during the war which began in 1756 [the " Seven Years' War" against France], in one of which, being stationed in the mizzen-top, he was carried overboard with the mast, but was taken up without having received any hurt. He was midshipman in the *Dolphin*, commanded by Commodore Byron, on her first voyage round the world [1764–1766], and afterwards served on the American station. In 1768 he made his second voyage round the world as master's mate in the *Endeavour* under Captain Cook, and by the promotion that took place during the expedition he returned as lieutenant. His third voyage round the world was in the *Resolution* [1772–1775], of which he was appointed the second lieutenant under Captain Cook; and soon after his return he was promoted to the rank of master and commander. When the present expedition was ordered to be fitted out, he was appointed to the *Discovery*, to accompany Captain

# G. A. HENTY

## When London Burned: A Story of Restoration Times. Illustrated by J. FINNEMORE. Olivine edges, 6s.

"A handsome volume, and boys will rejoice to possess it. . . ."—*Record.*

## – A March on London: A Story of Wat Tyler's Insurrection. Illustrated by W. H. MARGETSON. Olivine edges, 5s.

"The story of Wat Tyler's ever-famous insurrection is set forth with a degree of cunning that may always be looked for in the work that comes from this practised hand."—*Daily Telegraph.*

## – The Treasure of the Incas: A Tale of Adventure in Peru. Illustrated by WAL PAGET. With a Map. Olivine edges, 5s.

"The interest never flags for one moment, and the story is told with vigour."
—*World.*

## – With Roberts to Pretoria: A Tale of the South African War. Illustrated by WILLIAM RAINEY, R.I. With a Map. Olivine edges, 6s.

"In this story of the South African war Mr. Henty proves once more his incontestable pre-eminence as a writer for boys."—*Standard.*

## – Bonnie Prince Charlie: A Tale of Fontenoy and Culloden. Illustrated by GORDON BROWNE, R.I. Olivine edges, 6s.

"A historical romance of the best quality."—*Academy.*

## – Through Russian Snows: or, Napoleon's Retreat from Moscow. Illustrated by W. H. OVEREND. Olivine edges, 5s.

"The hero is altogether a fine character such as boys will delight in, whilst the story of the campaign is very graphically told."—*St. James's Gazette.*

## – The Tiger of Mysore: A Story of the War with Tippoo Saib. Illustrated by W. H. MARGETSON. Olivine edges, 6s.

"Mr. Henty not only concocts a thrilling tale, he weaves fact and fiction with so skilful a hand that the reader cannot help acquiring a just and clear view of that fierce and terrible struggle which gave to us our Indian empire."—*Athenæum.*

## – On the Irrawaddy: A Story of the First Burmese War. Illustrated by W. H. OVEREND. Olivine edges, 5s.

"Stanley Brooke's pluck is even greater than his luck, and he is precisely the boy to hearten with emulation the boys who read his stirring story."—*Saturday Review.*

resignation to his fate afforded them some consolation. It was impossible not to feel a more than common degree of compassion for a person whose life had been a continued scene of those difficulties and hardships to which a seaman's occupation is subject, and under which he at last sank.

He was brought up to the navy from his earliest youth, and had been in several actions during the war which began in 1756 [the "Seven Years' War" against France], in one of which, being stationed in the mizzen-top, he was carried overboard with the mast, but was taken up without having received any hurt. He was midshipman in the *Dolphin*, commanded by Commodore Byron, on her first voyage round the world [1764–1766], and afterwards served on the American station. In 1768 he made his second voyage round the world as master's mate in the *Endeavour* under Captain Cook, and by the promotion that took place during the expedition he returned as lieutenant. His third voyage round the world was in the *Resolution* [1772–1775], of which he was appointed the second lieutenant under Captain Cook; and soon after his return he was promoted to the rank of master and commander. When the present expedition was ordered to be fitted out, he was appointed to the *Discovery*, to accompany Captain

Cook; and, by the death of the latter, succeeded to the chief command.

It would be doing his memory extreme injustice not to say that during the short time the expedition was under his direction he was most zealous and anxious for its success.  His health, about the time the principal command devolved upon him, began to decline very rapidly, and was every way unequal to encountering the rigours of a high northern climate.  But the vigour and activity of his mind had in no shape suffered by the decay of his body; and though he knew that by delaying his return to a warmer climate he was giving up the only chance that remained for his recovery, yet, careful and jealous to the last degree that a regard to his own situation should never bias his judgment to the prejudice of the service, he persevered in the search of a passage till it was the opinion of every officer in both ships that it was impracticable, and that any further attempts would be not only fruitless but dangerous.

# Blackie & Son's
# Illustrated Story Books

*Large crown 8vo, cloth extra*

## G. A. HENTY

### Under Drake's Flag: A Tale of the Spanish Main. Illustrated. *New Edition.*
Olivine edges, 3s. 6d.

> "A stirring book of Drake's time, and just such a book as the youth of this maritime country are likely to prize highly."—*Daily Telegraph.*

### —Orange and Green: A Tale of the Boyne and Limerick. Illustrated. *New Edition.* Olivine edges, 3s. 6d.

> "*Orange and Green* is an extremely spirited story."—*Saturday Review.*

### —A Final Reckoning: A Tale of Bush Life in Australia. Illustrated. *New Edition.* Olivine edges, 3s. 6d.

> "Mr. Henty has never published a more readable, a more carefully constructed, or a better-written story than this."—*The Spectator.*

### —By Right of Conquest: or, With Cortez in Mexico. Illustrated. *New Edition.*
Olivine edges, 3s. 6d.

> "Mr. Henty's skill has never been more convincingly displayed than in this admirable and ingenious story."—*Saturday Review.*

### —With Cochrane the Dauntless: A Tale of his Exploits.
Illustrated. *New Edition.* Olivine edges, 3s. 6d.

> "This tale we specially recommend, for the career of Lord Cochrance and his many valiant fights in the cause of liberty deserve to be better known than they are."
> —*St. James's Gazette.*

### —A Jacobite Exile: or, In the Service of Charles XII of Sweden. Illustrated. *New Edition.* Olivine edges, 3s. 6d.

> "Shows Mr. Henty at his best. *A Jacobite Exile* is full of life, adventure, movement, and admirably illustrated."—*Scotsman.*

# G. A. HENTY

## With Frederick the Great: A Tale of the Seven Years' War. Illustrated. *New Edition.* Olivine edges, 3s. 6d.

"It is a good deal to say, but this prolific and admirable writer has never done better than this story."—*British Weekly.*

## – With Moore at Corunna: A Tale of the Peninsular War. Illustrated. *New Edition.* Olivine edges, 3s. 6d.

"A very spirited story."—*Spectator.*

## – Facing Death: or, The Hero of the Vaughan Pit. Illustrated. *New Edition.* Olivine edges, 3s. 6d.

"If any father, godfather, clergyman, or schoolmaster is on the lookout for a good book to give as a present to a boy who is worth his salt, this is the book we would recommend."—*Standard.*

## – The Dragon and the Raven: or, The Days of King Alfred. Illustrated. *New Edition.* Olivine edges, 3s. 6d.

"A well-built superstructure of fiction on an interesting substratum of fact."
—*Athenæum.*

## – One of the 28th: A Tale of Waterloo. Illustrated. *New Edition.* Olivine edges, 3s. 6d.

"Contains one of the best descriptions of the various battles which raged round Waterloo which it has ever been our fate to read."—*Daily Telegraph.*

## – Cat of Bubastes: A Story of Ancient Egypt. Illustrated. *New Edition.* Olivine edges, 3s. 6d.

"Full of exciting adventures."—*Saturday Review.*

## – With Clive in India: or, The Beginnings of an Empire. Illustrated. *New Edition.* Olivine edges, 3s. 6d.

"Those who know something about India will be the first to thank Mr. Henty for giving them this instructive volume to place in the hands of their children."
—*Academy.*

## – Condemned as a Nihilist: A Story of Escape from Siberia. Illustrated by WAL PAGET. *New Edition.* Olivine edges, 3s. 6d.

"His narrative is more interesting than many of the tales with which the public is familiar of escape from Siberia."—*National Observer.*

# G. A. HENTY

## Under Wellington's Command: A Tale of the Peninsular War. Illustrated by WAL PAGET. *New Edition.* Olivine edges, 3s. 6d.

"An admirable exposition of Mr. Henty's masterly method of combining instruction with amusement."—*World.*

## – The Young Carthaginian: A Story of the Times of Hannibal. Illustrated. *New Edition.* Olivine edges, 3s. 6d.

"From first to last nothing stays the interest of the narrative. It bears us along as on a stream, whose current varies in direction, but never loses its force."
—*Saturday Review.*

## – By England's Aid: or, The Freeing of the Netherlands (1585–1604). Illustrated by ALFRED PEARSE. With 4 Maps. *New Edition.* Olivine edges, 3s. 6d.

"Boys know and love Mr. Henty's books of adventure, and will welcome his tale of the freeing of the Netherlands."—*Athenæum.*

## – The Lion of the North: A Tale of Gustavus Adolphus. Illustrated. *New Edition.* Olivine edges, 3s. 6d.

"The tale is a clever and instructive piece of history, and as boys may be trusted to read it conscientiously, they can hardly fail to be profited as well as pleased."
—*The Times.*

## – The Lion of St. Mark: A Tale of Venice. Illustrated. *New Edition.* Olivine edges, 3s. 6d.

"Every boy should read *The Lion of St. Mark.*"—*Saturday Review.*

## – Both Sides the Border: A Tale of Hotspur and Glendower. Illustrated by RALPH PEACOCK. *New Edition.* Olivine edges, 3s. 6d.

"Mr. Henty retains the reader's interest throughout the story, which he tells clearly and vigorously."—*Daily Telegraph.*

## – Captain Bayley's Heir: A Tale of the Gold Fields of California. Illustrated. *New Edition.* Olivine edges, 3s. 6d.

"The portraits of Captain Bayley and the headmaster of Westminster School are admirably drawn, and the adventures in California are told with that vigour which is peculiar to Mr. Henty."—*Academy.*

# G. A. HENTY

## When London Burned: A Story of Restoration Times. Illustrated by J. FINNEMORE. Olivine edges, 6s.

"A handsome volume, and boys will rejoice to possess it. . . ."—*Record.*

## – A March on London: A Story of Wat Tyler's Insurrection. Illustrated by W. H. MARGETSON. Olivine edges, 5s.

"The story of Wat Tyler's ever-famous insurrection is set forth with a degree of cunning that may always be looked for in the work that comes from this practised hand."—*Daily Telegraph.*

## – The Treasure of the Incas: A Tale of Adventure in Peru. Illustrated by WAL PAGET. With a Map. Olivine edges, 5s.

"The interest never flags for one moment, and the story is told with vigour."
—*World.*

## – With Roberts to Pretoria: A Tale of the South African War. Illustrated by WILLIAM RAINEY, R.I. With a Map. Olivine edges, 6s.

"In this story of the South African war Mr. Henty proves once more his incontestable pre-eminence as a writer for boys."—*Standard.*

## – Bonnie Prince Charlie: A Tale of Fontenoy and Culloden. Illustrated by GORDON BROWNE, R.I. Olivine edges, 6s.

"A historical romance of the best quality."—*Academy.*

## – Through Russian Snows: or, Napoleon's Retreat from Moscow. Illustrated by W. H. OVEREND. Olivine edges, 5s.

"The hero is altogether a fine character such as boys will delight in, whilst the story of the campaign is very graphically told."—*St. James's Gazette.*

## – The Tiger of Mysore: A Story of the War with Tippoo Saib. Illustrated by W. H. MARGETSON. Olivine edges, 6s.

"Mr. Henty not only concocts a thrilling tale, he weaves fact and fiction with so skilful a hand that the reader cannot help acquiring a just and clear view of that fierce and terrible struggle which gave to us our Indian empire."—*Athenæum.*

## – On the Irrawaddy: A Story of the First Burmese War. Illustrated by W. H. OVEREND. Olivine edges, 5s.

"Stanley Brooke's pluck is even greater than his luck, and he is precisely the boy to hearten with emulation the boys who read his stirring story."—*Saturday Review.*

# G. A. HENTY

**Wulf the Saxon:** A Story of the Norman Conquest. Illustrated by RALPH PEACOCK.
Olivine edges, 6s.

> "We may safely say that a boy may learn from it more genuine history than he will from many a tedious tome."—*Spectator.*

— **With Kitchener in the Soudan:** A Tale of Atbara and Omdurman. Illustrated by W. RAINEY, R.I. With 3 Maps. Olivine edges, 6s.

> "Mr. Henty has collected a vast amount of information about the reconquest of the Soudan, and he succeeds in impressing it upon his reader's mind."—*Literary World.*

— **At the Point of the Bayonet:** A Tale of the Mahratta War.
Illustrated by WAL PAGET. With 2 Maps. Olivine edges, 6s.

> "A brisk, dashing narrative."—*Bookman.*

— **Through the Sikh War:** A Tale of the Conquest of the Punjaub.
Illustrated by HAL HURST. Olivine edges, 6s.

> "On the whole we have never read a more vivid and faithful narrative of military adventure in India."—*Academy.*

— **Through Three Campaigns:** A Story of Chitral, the Tirah, and Ashanti. Illustrated by WAL PAGET. With 3 Maps. Olivine edges, 6s.

> "Every true boy will enjoy this story of plucky adventure."—*Educational News.*

— **St. George for England:** A Tale of Cressy and Poitiers. Illustrated by GORDON BROWNE, R.I. Olivine edges, 5s.

> "A story of very great interest for boys."—*Pall Mall Gazette.*

— **With the British Legion:** A Story of the Carlist Wars. Illustrated by WAL PAGET. Olivine edges, 6s.

> "It is a rattling story told with verve and spirit."—*Pall Mall Gazette.*

— **True to the Old Flag:** A Tale of the American War of Independence.
Illustrated. Olivine edges, 6s.

> "Mr. Henty undoubtedly possesses the secret of writing eminently successful historical tales."—*Academy.*

# G. A. HENTY

## At Aboukir and Acre : Illustrated by WILLIAM RAINEY, R.I. Olivine edges, 5s.

"There is no doubt but that, for intrinsic interest and appropriateness, *At Aboukir and Acre* should rank high."—*Spectator.*

## – Redskin and Cow-Boy : A Tale of the Western Plains. Illustrated by ALFRED PEARSE. Olivine edges, 6s.

"A strong interest of open-air life and movement pervades the whole book."—*Scotsman.*

## – With Buller in Natal : or, A Born Leader. Illustrated by W. RAINEY, R.I., and a Map. Olivine edges, 6s.

"Just the sort of book to inspire an enterprising boy."—*Army and Navy Gazette.*

## – By Conduct and Courage : A Story of the Days of Nelson. Illustrated by WILLIAM RAINEY, R.I. Olivine edges, 6s.

"As it is the last it is good to be able to say that it shows no falling off in the veteran's vigour of style or in his happy choice of a subject."—*Globe.*

## – With the Allies to Pekin : A Story of the Relief of the Legations. Illustrated by WAL PAGET. With a Map. Olivine edges, 6s.

"The author's object being to interest and amuse, it must be admitted that he has succeeded."—*Guardian.*

## – By Sheer Pluck : A Tale of the Ashanti War. Illustrated by GORDON BROWNE, R.I. Olivine edges, 5s.

"Written with a simple directness, force, and purity of style worthy of Defoe."
—*Christian Leader.*

## – To Herat and Cabul : A Story of the First Afghan War. Illustrated by C. M. SHELDON. With Map. Olivine edges, 5s.

"We can heartily commend it to boys, old and young."—*Spectator.*

## – A Knight of the White Cross : A Tale of the Siege of Rhodes. Illustrated by RALPH PEACOCK. Olivine edges, 6s.

"In stirring interest this is quite up to the level of Mr. Henty's former historical tales."—*Saturday Review.*

(6)

# G. A. HENTY

## In the Heart of the Rockies: A Story of Adventure

in Colorado. Illustrated by G. C. HINDLEY. Olivine edges, 5s.

" Mr. Henty is seen here at his best as an artist in lightning fiction."—*Academy.*

## – The Bravest of the Brave: or, With Peterborough in Spain. With 8

page Illustrations by H. M. PAGET. Olivine edges, 5s.

" The adventures of the aide-de-camp, Jack, will probably be found to be no less interesting than the marvellous operations of the General himself, in which he takes a leading part."—*Spectator.*

## – A Roving Commission: or, Through the Black Insurrection of Hayti.

Illustrated by WILLIAM RAINEY, R.I. Olivine edges, 6s.

" A stirring tale, which may be confidently recommended to schoolboy readers."
—*Guardian.*

## – St. Bartholomew's Eve: A Tale of the Huguenot Wars. With Illustra-

tions and a Map. Olivine edges, 6s.

" A really good story."—*Bookman.*

## – For Name and Fame: or, To Cabul with Roberts. Illustrated. Olivine edges,

5s.

" The book teems with spirited scenes and stirring adventures."—*School Guardian.*

## – Maori and Settler: A Story of the New Zealand War. Illustrated by ALFRED

PEARSE. Olivine edges, 5s.

" A book which all young people, but especially boys, will read with avidity."
—*Athenæum.*

## – In the Reign of Terror: The Adventures of a Westminster Boy.

Illustrated by J. SCHÖNBERG. Olivine edges, 5s.

" May fairly be said to beat Mr. Henty's record."—*Saturday Review.*

## – Beric the Briton: A Story of the Roman Invasion of Britain. Illustrated by W. PAR-

KINSON. Olivine edges, 6s.

" He is a hero of the most attractive kind. . . . One of the most spirited and well-imagined stories Mr. Henty has written."—*Saturday Review.*

# G. A. HENTY

## No Surrender! A Tale of the Rising in La Vendée. Illustrated by STANLEY L. WOOD. Olivine edges, 5s.

"A vivid tale of manly struggle against oppression."—*World*.

## –The Dash for Khartoum: A Tale of the Nile Expedition. Illustrated by JOHN SCHÖNBERG and J. NASH. Olivine edges, 6s.

"It is literally true that the narrative never flags a moment."—*Academy*.

## –In Greek Waters: A Story of the Grecian War of Independence. Illustrated by W. S. STACEY. Olivine edges, 6s.

"There are adventures of all kinds for the hero and his friends, whose pluck and ingenuity in extricating themselves from awkward fixes are always equal to the occasion."—*Journal of Education*.

## –With Wolfe in Canada: or, The Winning of a Continent. Illustrations by GORDON BROWNE. Olivine edges, 6s.

"A moving tale of military exploit and thrilling adventure."—*Daily News*.

## –Out with Garibaldi: A Story of the Liberation of Italy. Illustrated by W. RAINEY, R.I. Olivine edges, 5s.

"It is a stirring tale."—*Graphic*.

## –Held Fast for England: A Tale of the Siege of Gibraltar. Illustrated by GORDON BROWNE. Olivine edges, 5s.

"There is no cessation of exciting incident throughout the story."—*Athenæum*.

## –Won by the Sword: A Tale of the Thirty Years' War. Illustrated by CHARLES M. SHELDON. Olivine edges, 6s.

"As fascinating as ever came from Mr. Henty's pen."—*Westminster Gazette*.

## –In the Irish Brigade: A Tale of War in Flanders and Spain. Illustrated by CHARLES M. SHELDON. Olivine edges, 6s.

"A stirring book of military adventure."—*Scotsman*.

## –At Agincourt: A Tale of the White Hoods of Paris. Illustrated by WAL PAGET. Olivine edges, 6s.

"Cannot fail to commend itself to boys of all ages."—*Manchester Courier*.

# Blackie & Son's
# Story Books for Boys

*Large crown 8vo, cloth extra.*  *Illustrated*

## Capt. F. S. BRERETON

**A Hero of Sedan:** A Tale of the Franco-Prussian War. Illustrated by STANLEY L. WOOD. Olivine edges, 6s.

> "Captain Brereton's deep knowledge of military tactics, together with his thorough acquaintance with and strict adherence to historical fact, are qualities which add importance to the writing of the book, the exciting events of which are developed in a manly spirit and healthy tone."—*Academy.*

**—John Bargreave's Gold:** A Tale of Adventure in the Caribbean. Illustrated by CHARLES M. SHELDON. Olivine edges, 5s.

> "There is a vigorous originality in the incidents that constitute the story. Those who like to be thrilled—and what boy does not?—will find all they want abundantly supplied."—*Glasgow Herald.*

**—How Canada was Won:** A Tale of Wolfe and Quebec. Illustrated by W. RAINEY, R.I. Olivine edges, 6s.

> "Here history and romance are blended, with the adeptness we expect of Captain Brereton, who is one of the best of living writers for boys."—*Birmingham Post.*

**—Roughriders of the Pampas:** A Tale of Ranch Life in South America. Illustrated by STANLEY L. WOOD. Olivine edges, 5s.

> "The interest is unflagging throughout the well-written tale."—*World.*

**—With Wolseley to Kumasi:** A Story of the First Ashanti War. Illustrated by GORDON BROWNE, R.I. Olivine edges, 6s.

> "The author's experiences enable him to depict warfare in the dark corners of the Empire with an accuracy of detail to be envied by most of his rivals."—*Outlook.*

**—Jones of the 64th:** A Tale of the Battles of Assaye and Laswaree. Illustrated by W. RAINEY, R.I. Olivine edges, 5s.

> "The story is full of dash and spirit, and betrays the military knowledge of the author."—*Birmingham Post.*

# Capt. F. S. BRERETON

## Roger the Bold : A Tale of the Conquest of Mexico. Illustrated. Olivine edges, 6s.

"The tale forms lively reading, the fighting being especially good."—*Athenæum.*

## – With Roberts to Candahar : A Tale of the Third Afghan War. Illustrated. Olivine edges, 5s.

"A very tried author, who improves with each book he writes, is Captain F. S. Brereton."—*Academy.*

## – A Knight of St. John : A Tale of the Siege of Malta. Illustrated. Olivine edges, 6s.

"Would enthral any boy reader."—*World.*

## – A Soldier of Japan : A Tale of the Russo-Japanese War. Illustrated. Olivine edges, 5s.

"The pages bristle with hairbreadth escapes and gallantry."—*Graphic.*

## – Foes of the Red Cockade : A Story of the French Revolution. Illustrated. Olivine edges, 6s.

"Captain Brereton describes their experiences with the vigour and spirit which always lend force to his writing."—*World.*

## – With Rifle and Bayonet : A Story of the Boer War. Illustrated. Olivine edges, 5s.

"The book is one the British boy will read and treasure."—*Newcastle Journal.*

## – With the Dyaks of Borneo : A Tale of the Head Hunters. Illustrated. Olivine edges, 6s.

"Young readers must be hard to please if *With the Dyaks* does not suit them."
—*Spectator.*

## – In the King's Service : A Tale of Cromwell's Invasion of Ireland. Illustrated. Olivine edges, 5s.

"The book is calculated to stir the pulses of all readers."—*Liverpool Courier.*

## – A Hero of Lucknow : A Tale of the Indian Mutiny. Illustrated. Olivine edges, 5s.

"Full of action and picturesque adventure."—*British Weekly.*

## – In the Grip of the Mullah : A Tale of Somaliland. Illustrated. Olivine edges, 5s.

"A fresher, more exciting, and more spirited tale could not be wished for."
—*British Weekly.*

# ALEXANDER MACDONALD

## Through the Heart of Tibet: A Tale of a Secret Mission to Lhasa.

Illustrated by WILLIAM RAINEY, R.I.   Olivine edges, 6s.

"A rattling story, told with Mr. Macdonald's usual verve and spirit."
—*British Weekly.*

## —The Hidden Nugget: A Story of the Australian Goldfields.   Illustrated by

WILLIAM RAINEY, R.I.   Olivine edges, 3s. 6d.

"It is a most breezy story, and life on a goldfield is well portrayed.  Peter the Poet is a happy study of a type to be found on all gold diggings."—*School Guardian.*

## —The White Trail: A Story of the Early Days of Klondike.   Illustrated by W.

RAINEY, R.I.   With a Map.   Olivine edges, 6s.

"One of the most powerful stories Mr. Macdonald has yet given his young readers."—*Glasgow Herald.*

## —The Island Traders: A Tale of the South Seas. Illustrated by CHARLES M.

SHELDON.   Olivine edges, 3s. 6d.

"The story is replete with excitement, which is well sustained throughout."
—*Teachers' Aid.*

## —The Pearl Seekers: A Story of Adventure in the Southern Seas.   Illustrated by

EDWARD S. HODGSON.   Olivine edges, 6s.

"This is the kind of story a boy will want to read at a sitting."—*Schoolmaster.*

## —The Quest of the Black Opals: A Story of Adventure

in the Heart of Australia.   Illustrated by W. RAINEY, R.I.   Olivine edges, 5s.

"An admirable tale."—*Westminster Gazette.*

## —The Lost Explorers: A Story of the Trackless Desert.   Illustrated by

ARTHUR H. BUCKLAND.   Olivine edges, 6s.

"As splendid and as vivid a narrative as any boy could wish to read."
—*Daily Graphic.*

# HARRY COLLINGWOOD

## The Cruise of the Thetis: A Tale of the Cuban Insurrection.   Illus-

trated by CYRUS CUNEO.   Olivine edges, 5s.

"We have, in Mr. Collingwood's book of adventure, not only a powerful but a well-written and unique story of the Cuban Insurrection.  From the first it grips and holds the full interest of the reader."—*Academy.*

# HARRY COLLINGWOOD

## Harry Escombe: A Tale of Adventure in Peru. Illustrated by VICTOR PROUT. Olivine edges, 3s. 6d.

> "The interest in this exciting tale of adventure in Peru never flags from beginning to end. . . . The account of Harry's journey to the City of the Sun, and his thrilling experiences there, will delight all those who revel in adventures."
> —*Practical Teacher.*

## —A Middy in Command: A Tale of the Slave Squadron. Illustrated by EDWARD S. HODGSON. Olivine edges, 6s.

> "A thoroughly good yarn of the right sort."—*Globe.*

## —Under the Chilian Flag: A Tale of the War between Chili and Peru (1879–1881). Illustrated by W. RAINEY, R.I. Olivine edges, 3s. 6d.

> "In *Under the Chilian Flag* Mr. Collingwood writes of naval warfare in a fashion likely to hold the close attention of any boy into whose hands the book may fall."
> —*Morning Post.*

# STAFF SURGEON T. T. JEANS, R.N.

## Ford of H.M.S. Vigilant: A Tale of Adventure in the Chusan Archipelago. Illustrated by W. RAINEY, R.I. Olivine edges, 5s.

> "In his latest volume Staff Surgeon Jeans has written a distinctly good story, and one feels safe in saying the worthy medico will soon be amongst the most popular of authors for youthful readers. He has a good style, knows what his readers require, and has the ability to retain interest throughout the story. As a gift book it is one of the best of its class."—*Naval and Military Record.*

## —Mr. Midshipman Glover, R.N.: A Tale of the Royal Navy of To-day. Illustrated by EDWARD S. HODGSON. Olivine edges, 5s.

> "Will probably prove one of the most successful boys' books of the season."
> —*Evening Standard.*

# HERBERT STRANG

## The Adventures of Harry Rochester: A Story of the Days of Marlborough and Eugene. Illustrated. Olivine edges, 6s.

> "One of the best stories of a military and historical type we have seen for many a day."—*Athenæum.*

# HERBERT STRANG

## Boys of the Light Brigade: A Story of Spain and the Peninsular War. Illustrated. Olivine edges, 6s.

Professor Oman (Chichele Professor of Modern History at Oxford, and author of *A History of the Peninsular War*) writes: "I can't tell you what a pleasure and rarity it is to the specialist to find a tale on the history of his own period in which the details are all right . . . accept thanks from a historian for having got historical accuracy combined with your fine romantic adventures".

## — Brown of Moukden: A Story of the Russo-Japanese War. Illustrated. Olivine edges, 5s.

"The book will hold boy readers spellbound."—*Church Times.*

## — Tom Burnaby: A Story of Uganda and the Great Congo Forest. Illustrated. Olivine edges, 5s.

"A delightful story of African adventure."—*Spectator.*

# ROBERT M. MACDONALD

## The Rival Treasure Hunters: A Tale of the Debatable Frontier of British Guiana. Illustrated. Olivine edges, 6s.

"A story which every schoolboy would probably describe as 'simply ripping'."
—*Daily Graphic.*

## — The Great White Chief: A Story of Adventure in Unknown New Guinea. Illustrated. Olivine edges, 6s.

"A rattling story told with spirit and vigour."—*British Weekly.*

# DAVID KER

## Under the Flag of France: A Tale of Bertrand du Guesclin. Illustrated. Olivine edges, 5s.

"One of the best stories of the season."—*Globe.*

## — Among the Dark Mountains: or, Cast away in Sumatra. Illustrated. Olivine edges, 3s. 6d.

"A glorious tale of adventure."—*Educational News.*

# ERNEST GLANVILLE

## The Diamond Seekers : A Story of Adventure in South Africa. Illustrated. Olivine edges, 6s.

"We have seldom seen a better story for boys."—*Guardian*.

## – In Search of the Okapi : A Story of Adventure in Central Africa. Illustrated. Olivine edges, 6s.

"An admirable story."—*Daily Chronicle*.

# MEREDITH FLETCHER

## Every Inch a Briton : A School Story. Illustrated. Olivine edges, 3s. 6d.

"In *Every Inch a Briton* Mr. Meredith Fletcher has scored a success."
—*Manchester Guardian*.

## – Jefferson Junior : A School Story. Illustrated. Olivine edges, 3s. 6d.

"A comical yarn."—*Yorkshire Daily Observer*.

# FREDERICK P. GIBBON

## The Disputed V.C. Illustrated by STANLEY L. WOOD. 3s.

"A good, stirring tale, well told."—*Graphic*.

# G. MANVILLE FENN

## Bunyip Land : Among the Blackfellows in New Guinea. Illustrated. 3s.

"One of the best tales of adventure produced by any living writer."
—*Daily Chronicle*.

## – In the King's Name. Illustrated. Olivine edges, 3s. 6d.

"This is, we think, the best of all Mr. Fenn's productions."—*Daily News*.

## – Dick o' the Fens : A Romance of the Great East Swamp. Illustrated by FRANK DADD. Olivine edges, 3s. 6d.

"We conscientiously believe that boys will find it capital reading."—*Times*.

# Dr. GORDON STABLES, R.N.

## The Naval Cadet: A Story of Adventure on Land and Sea. Illustrated. Olivine edges, 3s. 6d.

> "An interesting travellers' tale, with plenty of fun and incident in it."—*Spectator.*

## – For Life and Liberty: A Tale of the Civil War in America. With Illustrations and Map. 3s.

> "The story is lively and spirited, with abundance of blockade running, hard fighting, and narrow escapes."—*Times.*

## – To Greenland and the Pole: A Story of the Arctic Regions. Illustrated. 3s.

> "The adventures are actual experiences. It is one of the best books Dr. Stables has ever written."—*Truth.*

# FRED SMITH

## The World of Animal Life. A Natural History for Little Folk.

With eight full-page coloured Illustrations and numerous black-and-white Illustrations. Crown 4to, 11¼ inches by 9½ inches. Handsome cloth cover. Gilt top, 5s.

> "A volume that should be treasured as a reference book for the animal life of the world."—*Newcastle Journal.*

# A. J. CHURCH

## Lords of the World: A Tale of the Fall of Carthage and Corinth. Illustrated by RALPH PEACOCK. Olivine edges, 3s. 6d.

> "As a boys' book, *Lords of the World* deserves a hearty welcome."—*Spectator.*

# G. I. WHITHAM

## Sir Sleep-Awake and his Brother:

A Story of the Crusades. Illustrated by N. TENISON. 2s. 6d.

> "A stirring story that will hold the attention of young readers."—*Schoolmaster.*

# ESCOTT LYNN

## When Lion-Heart was King: A Tale of Robin Hood and Merry Sherwood. Illustrated. Olivine edges, 3s. 6d.

> "A lively tale of Robin Hood . . . certainly the adventures follow thick and fast."
> —*Birmingham Post.*

# CHARLES R. KENYON

## 'Twixt Earth and Sky: A Tale of Adventure in Central America.

Illustrated by CHARLES HORRELL. Olivine edges, 3s. 6d.

"A capital story of adventure."—*Globe.*

# DOROTHEA MOORE

## The Luck of Ledge Point: A Tale of 1805. Illustrated. 2s. 6d.

"We have tested the healthy excitement stimulated by the book on both a boy and a girl, and have found that the pages of this cleverly-told story appealed to both alike; consequently, we thoroughly recommend it as a gift book."—*Schoolmaster.*

## —God's Bairn: A Story of the Fen Country. Illustrated. Gilt edges, 3s. 6d.

"An excellent tale, most dainty in execution and fortunate in subject."—*Globe.*

# WALTER C. RHOADES

## For the Sake of His Chum: A School Story. Illustrated by N. TENISON. Olivine edges, 3s. 6d.

"There is a breeziness about the book which is sure to commend it."—*Athenæum.*

## —Two Scapegraces: A School Story. Illustrated by HAROLD COPPING. Olivine edges, 3s. 6d.

"A school story of high merit."—*Liverpool Mercury.*

# PAUL DANBY

## The Red Army Book. With many Illustrations in colour and in black-and-white. Olivine edges, 6s.

"Every boy would glory in the keeping and reading of such a prize."—*Daily Telegraph.*

# J. CUTHBERT HADDEN

## The Nelson Navy Book. With many Illustrations in colour and in black-and-white. Olivine edges, 6s.

"A stirring, heartening tale, bold and bracing as the sea itself."—*The Standard.*

# R. STEAD

## Kinsman and Namesake: A Story of the Days of Henry IV. Illustrated. 2s. 6d.

"Teems with exciting adventures."—*School Guardian.*